# Hold On Tight

## A son’s memoir of maternal attachment.

# Hold On Tight

## A son's memoir of maternal attachment.

Dominic J White

*Nostoi*

First published in Great Britain in 2015 by Nostoi Publishing.



Nostoi Publishing, Great Britain

Edited by Dr Mark Stibbe

Cover Design by Nostoi Graphic

Artwork by Abigail Jones Art

ISBN 978 0 993 20503 3

Printed and Bound in Great Britain by Caligraving, Norfolk

This book is an account of real events written by the same person who experienced them. It has been written with the aid of memory as well as case records as supplied by Derbyshire County Council. Some names have been changed in order to protect the identity of people mentioned including professionals who worked with the writer at the time these events occurred. Some location names have also been substituted by fictitious place and street names for similar reasons. Any resemblance of substituted names to actual persons, living or dead, or substituted locales to real locales, is entirely coincidental

A CIP catalogue record of this book is available from the British Library

# DEDICATION

I dedicate this book to all the women in my life
who hold on to me.
To my wife, my two daughters, my three sisters.
To my second mum, and my mother-in-law.
And to my mum, holding on to the
loving memory of you.

# ACKNOWLEDGEMENTS

I would like to thank my family, especially my wife and daughters, for allowing me the time and space to complete the journey of writing this book. I would also like to thank other family members for assisting me by generously supplying precious photographs and enriching accounts of my early life.

I would also like to thank friends and work colleagues who have supported me by reading and commenting upon my work, particularly those who have provided me with the great and essential service of proofreading.

My acknowledgements and thanks are also extended to individuals within Derbyshire County Council for reading my work, giving me feedback, and for furnishing me with my Care Records in the first instance.

Finally, I would like to thank all of the Social Workers who have helped me along the way, both in my childhood and my adulthood. You are an amazing bunch of people who change the world every day for people like me.

# CONTENTS

# PROLOGUE: TO MY MUM

Although I have no memory of it, I know I first met you when I was within your womb. I ate what you ate, smoked what you smoked and even heard your music. I lived all my waking and sleeping hours inside your body listening to your heartbeat. My tiny, grasping fingers grew and developed as the rush of your blood nourished me.

Despite the tightness of your umbilical cord around my neck, my birth heralded an unnatural distance between us - untold miles and three years. As a baby left in the care of another, I reached out with my hands and all my senses to lay claim to a maternal heart. I found a mother, although it was not you. Through her proximity I bonded as skin touched skin repeatedly, day after day and night after night. My growing brain absorbed all the love-drugs my body released to wash over it – oxytocin and dopamine bombs exploding as skin touched and eyes met - but not your skin, not your eyes. You were far away when I was bonding. I did not find you when I laid claim to a maternal heart. You were distant, unreachable, unknown.

Then you finally came to love me like a strange breeze, with your curls of dark hair and your green eyes. The promise of you captivated me as I reached for this new mother-heart with hands formed within your womb. I reached out to touch your skin through which I had first seen daylight when it was stretched tightly over me.

You warned me that this would be a long journey through a dark night. You told me what I needed to do to stay close to you.

'Hold on tight.'

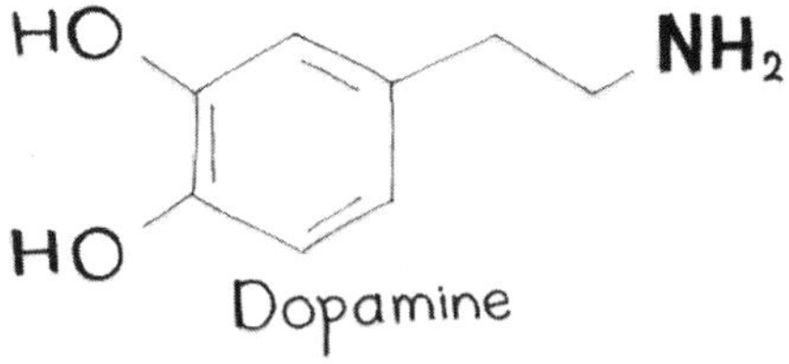

HO $NH_2$

HO

Dopamine

Attachment is a deep and enduring emotional bond that connects one person to another across time and space.

(*Ainsworth*, 1973; *Bowlby*, 1969).

Attachment does not have to be reciprocal.

(*Bowlby*, 1969).

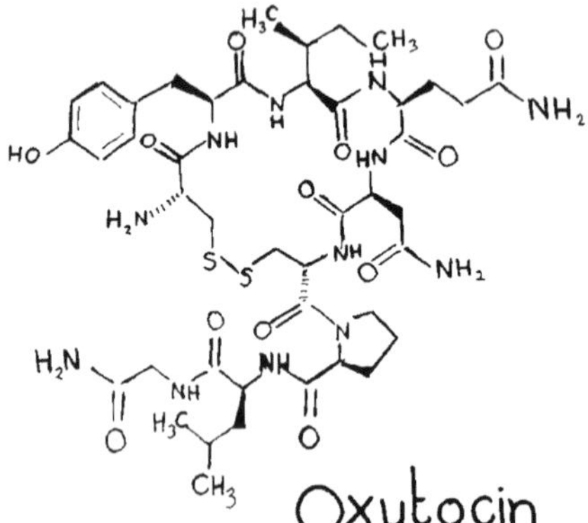

Oxytocin

1

# PLACE OF SAFETY

- London Borough of Lambeth
- Admitted on 23.02.1985
- PLACE OF SAFETY (POLICE)
- Attitude on admission: Pleasant but very hungry
- Appearance (physical): Very tired looking
- Appearance (dress): Tidy
- Age: 13
- Height: 5ft 4in
- Weight: 9st 4lb
- Build: Sturdy
- Complexion: Fresh
- Hair Colour: Mid-brown
- Eye Colour: Brown
- Face: Oval
- Ears: Close to head
- Nose: Ordinary
- Peculiarities: (Blank)
- By: Receiving Officer

*

My mum flew out of the kitchen with a long silver knife in her soft hand and a look of burning hatred in her green eyes. I turned and weaved through my two knee-high sisters on the way to my bedroom at the other end of the corridor, without looking back. It was as if I was in one of those dreams where you can't run fast enough – moving through treacle, not air. Something passed my ear and clunked against the wall. I saw the knife clatter to the tile floor as I strained towards the safest side of my plywood bedroom door.

As I pushed the door closed, I caught a brief glimpse of my two sisters, wide-eyed and open-mouthed in the hall. They had the look of excitement that you see when kids are playing 'what time is it Mr Wolf?'. I leaned my weight against the door, pushing it as hard shut as I could.

'You little swine, you damn little swine! I'm gonna kill you'. Mum banged the door as she fell onto it, pushing it open a hand-span. I pushed back as my trainers squeaked on the tiles. Again and again she pushed, causing the door to open every time she slammed her body weight against it. I resisted, my shoulder against hers. Then the knife jingled as it was picked back up and then thud, thud, thud, thud. I could feel the strikes of the knife echo through the wood into my palms. Mum stabbed the wood with diminishing force, her spiky words trailing off into wailing and sobbing. As she wept, the knife clattered once more to the floor. I breathed, and then slid to the floor. Love had become hate now, and comfort replaced by a sense of danger.

When I thought Mum had gone, I opened the door a crack to check. I could hear her sobs from her bedroom at the other end of the flat. I dared to open my door and reach. I grabbed the blade, briefly glancing up at the wood which had taken the force of Mum's attack. I saw untidy slits, four maybe five, with splinters protruding. I threw the knife onto my bed and then quickly barricaded my door as best as I could with a chest of draws and a chair. At least I would hear the furniture vibrating on the tiles if anyone tried to get into my room. I placed the plundered weapon under my pillow where it was safe. It looked too long, and too sharp, to be in a bedroom. I listened carefully to the sounds of the room, the house, the block, as I drifted into an uneasy sleep. I dreamt that Mum tried to kill me with a long, silver knife.

*

In the morning I went out, and later made myself return. I had been to see M&M, the youth workers who lived across the road in the flat at the top of the Methodist Church. There was an uneasy stillness between me and my mum. Our conversation was functional at first.

'Where have you been?'

'Here's your tea.'

'Don't forget the washing up.'

There was an elephant in the flat called 'you chased me with a knife last night and I thought you were going to kill me.'

After tea, I sat in my room and practised chords

Em, G and C on the nylon-stringed guitar M&M had leant to me. My door was closed but I was still listening with one ear. When Mum suddenly appeared around the door I looked at her hands – both visible with no knife, but my heart still pounded. I remained sitting on my bed with the guitar on my lap in front of me, my muscles tensed.

'What did your Christian friends have to say today then?'

'Nothing,' I replied.

'Did you tell them? Did you cry like a mardy-boy to them? *Ooo, Mummy chased me with a knife!* What did they say?'

'I didn't tell them.'

'Yes you did you little liar! You tell them everything, I know you do.'

'No I don't.'

Mum was ready to talk about what had happened. I knew she must have been sorry, or embarrassed, for what she had done. She had never used a knife before. I knew she was scared of other people knowing that she really lost it with me sometimes, especially M&M.

'I don't want you to see them anymore. They've brainwashed you. I'm gonna take that guitar back. I don't want anything of theirs in my house. Give me the guitar.'

Mum reached forward and grabbed it. The thought of losing my guitar was unbearable. I just didn't want Mum taking it back to them, spitting nails. I held on tightly, wrapping my arm around the smooth wooden body whilst gripping the neck with my other hand.

'Mum, I'll take it back. Let me take it...'

'Gimme the guitar! Give it to me now!'

Mum pulled harder, with yanking tugs. I shuffled backward across my squeaky metal bed, digging my heels into the mattress as my back pushed against the wall. The bed moved forwards, stopping at Mum's shins as I fell into the gap between the bed and the wall which opened up behind me. Mum let go and started to swear as she moved around the foot of my bed and pushed it aside to regain access to me and the guitar. Her face was now above mine as she straddled over me, gripping the guitar and trying to shake me off it. Her lips were twisted into a grimace, her teeth bared with the effort. I was lying on the floor underneath her, losing my grip.

Finally, my fingers gave way as Mum prised the guitar from my hands.

'Give it back," I said. "Give it back!'

'*Give it back! Give it back!* You sound like a girl.'

Mum's green eyes widened. She gripped the neck of the guitar with both hands and raised it for a strike. It hovered for a second over her head before it arced down onto me. As I turned to avoid the blow the side of the guitar hit my shoulder. It felt unreal. I couldn't believe Mum had just hit me with a guitar. She pushed the bed out further as I cowered in a foetal position on the floor with my arms and elbows out in front of me. Again the guitar came down, this time flat side as it twanged and resonated. The sound of Mum's accidental guitar playing, and my breathless song of pain, filled the room. And again the guitar swung down. This time I felt the wood give way and heard it splitting as my shoulder and elbow took the force of the blow. And again. And again. The final blow was more like the sweep of a mace as the broken end of the body, still attached to the neck by most of the strings, banged weakly onto my head. Mum stood over me, the remains of the broken guitar dangling from one hand. She looked mad, and satisfied. She was breathless, mouth open to catch the air. I heard my sisters crying and wailing in the hall.

Mum left me with the wreck of my guitar, dropping the wood onto the floor at my feet. I watched her back, clenching my teeth and squinting my eyes into slits as she left my bedroom. Suddenly I knew. I knew that now, right now, I had to leave.

I shoved as many clothes into the black bin-bag as I could. My shoulder and arm began to hurt, and the side of my head felt grazed. My dirty socks got stuffed in with the clean T-shirts. In went books: The Lord of the Rings, The Hobbit. I pulled away a photo blue-tacked onto my bedroom wall above my bed. It was a picture of me, with my arms crossed in a Kung-Fu pose on a Jamaican beach with the sea behind me sparkling in the sun. Mum had clicked open the camera shutter with a smile on her lips on a much happier day. I held it between finger and thumb. Part of me wanted to rip it up and part of me wanted to disappear back into it to find the smiling, sun-kissed woman. I looked at it through freshly brimming tears, then pushed it into the back pocket of my jeans.

Holding the bag at my knees, I cautiously opened my bedroom door and stepped into the hall. The bathroom door stood open opposite and the light was on, illuminating the hand-painted leaves and vines on its green walls. My sisters watched me from their bedroom as I moved towards the front door. I did not want to leave them, but that was now my plan. I could not remain in the same house as Mum. I could no longer bear the hatred pouring from her eyes. I did not feel safe.

Mum was stood at the door of the kitchen, half in, half out, and I could not see both of her hands. The front door stood closed, right opposite the kitchen. The door was either double locked or not; I could not tell from where I stood in the hall. I glanced at my sisters, at the door, at Mum. My worry was that Mum would become desperate when she realised I was serious about leaving.

'If you go, you can stay gone. You're not coming snivelling back this time. If you go, then that's it.'

This was hopeful; it meant that Mum would probably let me leave without any resistance.

I had never packed my own stuff before. I had never wanted to leave my mum enough to actually do it. Over the years it had been the opposite; I had clung onto my mum in every way I could, both when she was there for me, and when she was not. But on this day – 23rd February 1985, two months before my 14th Birthday – I was choosing to leave her and choosing to abandon my sisters. Fear was my engine, and self-preservation now became my desired destination.

I opened my arms to hug my sisters, which turned out instantly to be a bad move.

'Don't you dare upset them anymore,' Mum shouted. 'If you're gonna leave then just leave. Go on. Take your stuff and go. But if you leave, I'm not having you back this time. Ever.'

Mum disappeared into the kitchen. This was my chance. I called my sisters by name and told them that I loved them, then made for the door. I willed Mum to stay in the kitchen. I opened the front door, relieved that it was not double-locked. I ignored the slow, smelly lift and leaped down three floors worth of stairs with my heart thumping in my head. It felt like Mum was right behind me all the way down, but I knew she wasn't. My back straightened as I stepped through the last door at the bottom into the open space of the forecourt leading onto Wandsworth Road. As I looked behind me back up to the kitchen window, I saw the outline of my Mum turn away and disappear from view. Then I looked across the street to the blue doors of the Methodist Church, and then up to the two round stone turrets of M&M's flat at the top of the building. I felt like I was in one of Mum's favourite Paul Simon songs, who said there must be at least fifty ways to leave your lover.

# 2

# MARY OF SHARDLOW

'Mother very agitated and impulsive – May need psychiatric help.'

Derby Social Services on 27th March 1977.

*

Mum was twenty seven when a social worker made the above observation about her. I was nearly six. By that point in her life she had survived many tough experiences. My reflection as an adult, and as her son, is that help could have come a lot sooner.

Mary White was born on 6th August 1949. She was the daughter of Bernard Ronald White, otherwise known to friends and family as 'Ron', and Eileen Oldham, who became Mrs Eileen White in 1944, one year before World War II ended. I remember seeing a large black-and-white print of Ron and Eileen in military uniform when I was younger. She was sitting with him standing behind her, smiling beneath his Captain Scarlett hat.

Eileen's parents lived in the curious parish of Shardlow, which spans the South Derbyshire countryside beneath Derby and Nottingham. Most of

Eileen's seven siblings settled in, or around, the small, sleepy village of Melbourne. When I looked up Mum's family history on her mother's side, I felt like I was discovering an unseen heritage for me, and my sisters, and for Mum. Suddenly, there they all were, names, birth dates, death dates, marriage years: Kathleen born 1911; Thomas born 1913; William born 1914; Ivy born 1920; Joseph born 1921; Eileen (my grandma) born 1922; Antony born 1924; Mary born 1926. On the Oldham throne I found Thomas Oldham, born 1886, and Charlotte Tilson, also born in 1886. Charlotte and Thomas married in December 1906, and the rest is history.

Mum told me that she was very close to her nan Charlotte. I have a photograph of Mum and Charlotte together. Mum looks about three and wears a white bonnet whilst beaming the biggest toddler smile, with Nanny Charlotte stood behind her looking remarkably similar to Mum in later life. I can see everything good about Mum in that toddler smile, untainted by disappointments. I can see no trace of sorrow, or bitterness, in her beautiful face, only joy and fun. Today, when I look at that happy little person, I realise that I could have done more to help. *I could have tried to look after you better Mum, I should have. I wasn't strong enough for you.*

Charlotte died when Mum was aged twelve or thirteen. Mum told me that her nan's death had a big impact on her, bringing confusion and anger. Mum described herself as becoming 'rebellious' after her Nan's death, and that no-one understood how she felt at the time. I have seen the effect that the death of a close, beloved relative can have on a teenager's life in my work, especially when grief remains ignored and unresolved. Some children sink into quietness and sadness, some become sullen and angry.

Mum was already angry with Eileen and Ron for allowing her to eat too many sweets. She blamed them for her being overweight at an early age. She also blamed them for not protecting her. Mum had only ever spoken to me about the incident once. A man, in a tool shed, in the woods.

Mum said that when she was a teenager she went to 'Borstal', where according to her, she got high on sniffing wood glue while making furniture. Borstal was a bit like prison for teenagers and was an earlier, seemingly less secure version of the modern-day Youth Offending Institution. Mum claimed to have run away on occasions, which I can completely imagine her doing. The best answer I ever got from Mum about why she had been placed in Borstal was that she had been misbehaving - 'normal things that teenagers get up to.'

'Like what Mum?'

'Stealing, fighting, running away.'

Mum always described herself as 'the black sheep of the family', and had in practice distanced herself from the Oldham clan. I knew one great aunt, Aunt Mary, and a second cousin, but until recently I was ignorant regarding the whole extent of the family. I wonder how many of the clan saw her as Mary the lost sheep, not the black one.

As newly-weds, Ron and Eileen entered the Haberdashery business, setting up shop in Derby with needles, thread, buttons, materials and zips. Ron, Eileen and young Mary then moved house to a corner shop – newsagents and tobacconists – on the bottom of Martin Street in Derby. This shop no doubt was the source of sweets for Mum and tobacco for Ron and Eileen. Mum was raised living first above a sewing shop, then a sweet shop, both in a town not too far by car from green Shardlow or sleepy Melbourne, but the open countryside and the bluebell woods were too far away to see from young Mary's bedroom window. Sometimes when I spoke to Mum about her life in Derby I got the feeling that she would rather have stayed in Melbourne.

I never asked Mum enough about her childhood, or her teens. Something was 'broken' inside me, which held me back from spending enough time with her like this when she was alive. If she were alive today I would sit with her and ask her question after question, and ply her with cups of sweet milky tea. I would ask and ask, and write and write, pages and pages. I want to know more about what it was like for her, what she found joyful, hurtful, hard. I would ask her how she felt when she sat in a bluebell wood, or by the river Trent. I would ask her what dreams she had as a smiling child, both sleeping and waking.

*Mary of Shardlow, what scents did the wooded breeze bring you?*
*What sights filled your eyes?*
*Mary of Shardlow, what flavour sweets did they bring you?*
*Did you watch the moon in the night skies?*
*Mary of Shardlow, can you remember beyond sorrow and grief?*
*Can you see a time before death?*
*Or has Father Time been a thief?*

I would write poems for her, and songs. I would seek to know her, to discover who she was, what she felt. Now her experiences are lost to me and to future generations. Apart from the ones I and my sisters know about of course.

I would read you my poems, and write down yours. I would sing you my songs, and listen to yours. I would speak peace into your life while you lived it, to try and still the raging storms inside you. I would place ointment onto your wounds and sooth you with my hands. I would speak my love into your face and let you see into my heart. I would let you love me again. I would let you hold me for longer than I could bear. I would be strong for you, I would be present. But now those years are gone, leaving only my words of peace spoken softly to you in your final hour.

*

By the time Mum was twenty-one years old she had left the sweet shop and the Borstal and was living in a flat in Derby with a sixty year old taxi driver called Ted. Ted had left his own wife to be with Mary, and Mary was pregnant with me. Mum had just ended a summer love affair with a young Greek-Cypriot waiter. It was 1970 and Elvis was crooning with 'The Wonder of You' while The Kinks were l-la la-ing 'Lola.'

I entered the world three weeks overdue on 23rd April 1971, narrowly escaping death with my mother's umbilical cord stuck around my neck during birth. According to Mum, and my medical notes, I had to be rescued with forceps and literally pulled into the world by my head. I never asked Mum what she did with me the day I was born – if she held me, or looked into my eyes and smiled. What I do know from Mum is that she was not ready for me when I came. She was still young and by her own description she was a 'wild child' of the 60s. Mum had experienced the hippie revolution of love and psychedelic drugs while passing through her teenage years and had made many of the lifestyle choices popularised by the movement. Having a screaming, needy baby who was dependent on her for food, warmth and nurture was too much responsibility, too soon. In the summer of 1971, Mum loved her baby but from a distance.

I was bottle fed, but not by Mum, or Ted, or even the Greek-Cypriot waiter. Ted was not sold on the idea of having a baby at his age and had tried, according to Mum, to convince her to have an abortion. Mum leaned heavily on her own parents to help with looking after me as soon as I was born. I think this is usual, and natural, for a woman experiencing motherhood for the first time. They say that the first three months of sleepless nights is all about survival for the parents. Mum told me that she would leave me with her mother for hours, days, and weeks, which then turned into months. Before long I cried when Mum tried to hold me, not recognising who she was.

I have one very faint memory of a family drama involving Mum and my grandparents. Mum was shouting and Grandma was crying as she held me. Granddad was speaking with both hands raised palms down, trying to protect Grandma from Mum's fury. Granddad told Mum to leave, which she did with a slam of the front door. Mum always said that Eileen had emotionally blackmailed her by saying that she would die if Mum ever took me away from her. Mum used to have some large photographs of Grandma, Granddad and I. I once asked Mum to send them to me in the post, which she did, with all the images of Grandma cut out, leaving jagged Grandma-shaped holes. Mum said that Grandma had stolen me away from her.

Mum's early adult life is mostly a mystery to me. I know that she was a passenger in a car crash in which the driver of the car died. She said that she saw the dead man again in a dream. In the dream he took her to a big house and said, 'Let me show you. There are many rooms.' Mum's nose was broken in the accident, which left a small scar and a slight crookedness. There was lots of glass flying around in the crash and many years later Mum felt that some of the glass was re-emerging from the skin on her arms. She would scratch and scratch.

I also know that Mum started to smoke cannabis and to take speed and LSD in her mid-teens. There was a story she would tell of emerging from a pub with some friends and seeing all the lampposts as Tripod spacecraft from *The War of the Worlds* and feeling pretty scared.

I have no idea how 'wild' Mum was when she was with Ted in the early years, apart from hints from my own care records that suggested being with Ted somehow curtailed the more adventurous aspects of Mum's lifestyle. I know she had tattoos – a green snake on her leg, words on her arms. She liked motorbikes and people who rode them. I'm not sure how she felt about taxis.

I know that she visited family in Melbourne often as a child, but I am not sure if she kept this up in her teens. The distance from Martin Street in Derby to Melbourne is not great, but the emotional distance for Mum, was vast. Mary of Shardlow, who loved bluebells, woods, and rivers, became Mary of Derby, who needed to maintain distance between herself and those she felt had hurt her.

By the time I arrived in her world, three weeks late, Mum was out on a distant limb and far away from her family roots. The Greek-Cypriot waiter was apparently asking about me. The taxi driver had by this time stopped trying to convince Mum to kill me. And Mum, well, she had faithfully carried me to term, and beyond, in her bulging tummy. I wish I could write more about her nine month adventure of carrying me, and feeding me in her inmost parts. I would love to know who she was with, what she did, what emotions she felt as they washed over me. If I could play back the compact disc of what I heard, or the Blu-ray of what I saw through Mum's thinly-stretched skin, I wonder what that would look like. Mum somehow got us both through those nine months and three weeks safely. With the help of quick-thinking medical staff she delivered me into the world alive and kicking.

Whether by gut instinct or purposeful decision, Mum then chose to leave me in the safest place possible. My days of comfort and nurture in the homely house of Ron and Eileen White, my most beloved grandparents, were about to begin.

# 3

# GRANDMA'S SKIN

'Was in the care of grandparents for the first three years of his life: Maternal grandparents deceased 1975. Mother has a history of psychiatric illness and drug taking.'

Derby Social Services 1977.

*

I sit on Grandma's knee. She is beautiful, and we watch Andy Pandy together. Grandma's face is pretty, framed by soft curls of brown hair. As I sit in her cuddle my hand reaches up to grasp her soft earlobe between my forefinger and thumb. I rub her ear gently, drawing comfort from the smoothness and softness of its feel. Her smell is just like how a mother should smell.

I drink a glass of milk and eat my Jaffa cake – chocolate coating first, then the sponge topped with orange jelly. I go through the round window with Big Ted from Playschool on the telly, to a factory where they make thousands of sweeties and put them on a conveyor belt. I hear Grandma singing in the kitchen behind the bead-curtain. Megan the chocolate-brown poodle, who smells doggy and damp, spins round and round on the same patch of rug in front of the fireplace – round and round and round, before she finally collapses in a heap with a long sigh.

I hear barking coming from the backyard. I jump up and brush past the bead-curtain into the kitchen to greet Mick the dog at the back door as Grandma lets him in. Mick looks as big as a horse with his dark, short fur and huge muscled shoulders. We greet each other eye-to-eye, me patting him hard and him sniffing my face.

Grandma smiles and rubs my head, and then puts Mick's food bowl onto the floor. She has an apron on with a floral pattern, framed with white frills around the edge. As I sit back down in front of the fire I stroke Megan, who sighs and sniffs, and then rolls over to present her pink belly for me to rub.

*

Grandma opens the front door and tips my buggy over the threshold and out of the cold wind. She takes my coat off and rubs my cheeks. I help Grandma lay the table at the back end of the lounge with cutlery and sauces. Then she sits on the floor with me and takes her headscarf off. I feel her smooth, cold skin, fresh from the bluster of the wind outside. My fingers trace the smile lines at the corner of her eyes, trailing into her hair. She pulls out her round pearl earrings so that I can rub her smooth earlobe.

Suddenly I hear the front door being opened – the key scratching and then turning; the door creaking open, and then being shut. From the floor, still in Grandma's embrace, I look up to the small window into the hall. I know who I will soon see any second now. Granddad's grinning face appears briefly, and then disappears, to my squeals of delight. Then again. This time I jump up and point to his face peering through the window down at me. As I look back to Grandma she smiles at me, and then him, with twinkling eyes.

The smell of chips and vinegar wafts into the room as Granddad enters and gives me a hug. He sits down at the table and opens the wrap of white, greasy paper. He sits me on his knee as he spots Daddies Sauce onto his chips, perfect spaces apart. Then he pats out a dollop of Heinz Tomato Ketchup at the side of his plate, especially for me. He looks away purposefully, giving me the cue to steal a chip, which I do. The chip-stealing game continues happily until he is ready to read his newspaper and finish off the remains of his fish and chip supper. Grandma emerges from the kitchen with a cup of tea in her hand which she places on the table next to Granddad's plate.

*

Granddad is sitting on the sofa, reading a newspaper. I am playing with my teddy on the carpet by his feet. My teddy seems bigger than me;

it has long floppy tube-like arms and legs and a neat, pointed nose. It's a great teddy, all brown and soft and furry. Granddad puts down his paper and puts my teddy in a tall box. We open the box, and find my teddy inside! Granddad lays the tall box on its side and we pull teddy out. Then I climb into the box and Granddad makes sure teddy follows me in. He smiles, and closes the lid at the top of the box. His face disappears and it goes darker, but I can still see teddy and the inside of the cardboard box.

Suddenly I panic and push with my hands at the flaps of the box. They move but don't open. Now I feel trapped, and the air gets harder to breath. I cry and gasp for air as the flaps suddenly open and Granddad pulls me out. He smiles and says, "Ah, there now. It's all right. You're out now. Do you want teddy out too?"

He pulls teddy out of the box, and then he smacks the box.

'Naughty box', he says.

*

The Tardis whizzes through pulsating space on the telly and Doctor Who appears with a big stripy scarf. I sit watching with Granddad while Grandma waits at the side of the settee – I know that it's nearly time for bed.

'You'll get scared young man. You'll be behind the sofa in a minute.'

'No Grandma.'

'Yes you will.'

Then the Daleks arrive. They have bobbles on their robot shells, and a single eye on a wiggly stick at the front of their face. I stay on the sofa, snuggling close to Granddad, until the Daleks' ears light up and they speak in a scary metallic voice.

'EXTERMINATE! EXTERMINATE!'

I leap up and run to the back of the sofa and hide. After a while I stand back up and peak over the top of the sofa and Granddad's shoulder.

'I think it's time for bed young man.'

Grandma takes my hand and pulls me from behind the sofa. I kiss Granddad goodnight and then we open the door to the stairs. I wave to Granddad and I go up the stairs with Grandma behind me, up the apples and pears, to sleepy-land.

*

Grandma and I go shopping together. When we go through the till at the end she lets me lick the green stamps with a shield on them and stick them in her book. Then we go around the market together looking at the fruit, and the fish.

On the way home we stop at the corner shop at the top of Martin Street with the picture of two children playing together eating 'Lyons Ice-cream'. Grandma buys some Camp Coffee and I look into the glass cabinet at the bottom and choose some black-jack chews and a flying saucer.

When we get home I sit on the carpet next to

Megan the poodle, playing with a metal clasp with shiny stones on it that expands when you pull it out. Then Grandma lets me sniff the holes of a round, white porcelain pomander with a rose pattern on it, which smells of flowers.

*

I sit in the warmth of the sun on the soft back seat of the car, peering into the front and sticking my face between Grandma and Granddad in the front seats. We are in a traffic queue and the sun is shining in the blue sky. I can see the glinting ridges at the front of the car where the headlights are, and the silver wing mirror which sticks out beside Granddad's window. We are now approaching a gate and Granddad speaks to a man in a window and gives him some tickets. We drive slowly on to the chalet and I sit on a grey blanket on the grass outside while they unpack.

I climb onto the ride, which goes around to music and talks to me as I cling onto the hard plastic monkey-like Dr Seuss character. Then we walk along the beachfront in the sun, looking at the men playing music on accordions and a piano. A man with a monkey on a lead comes over to us but I hide behind Granddad, afraid of the screeching creature.

I run around in a circle on a windy beach getting hot in a coat with the string hood pulled tight around my face, and Grandma chases me. When she catches me she falls to her knees and starts to dig with a spade. I grab her face and kiss her on her soft cheek. Granddad kneels down on one knee and clicks his camera, smiling from behind the lens.

Then I am sitting on the sand with a bucket and spade, digging a hole. I know Grandma is near, but I cannot see her. I am slightly worried by this but happy to dig on down. Suddenly a girl appears. She grabs my ears in her hands and shakes my head back and forth as she grins into my face. She has dark curly hair and chubby cheeks. My ears hurt, and I pull her fingers away from them and cry. As she walks off smiling, I get up and look for Grandma, spinning round and around in the sunshine. Out of nowhere she sweeps me up in her arms and rubs my stinging ears.

Again we walk along the seafront, me swinging in-between Grandma and Granddad as they haul me up into the air by my hands.

*

I sit on Grandma's knee in the living room. She is sitting on a tall-backed chair and coughing black spit into a handkerchief. She is crying, and coughing, and crying.

Granddad is not here anymore, and I feel the space he has left empty in this moment. I look at Grandma helplessly as she coughs loudly, her shoulders shaking.

When she finally stops coughing, I feel the skin on Grandma's throat, and ask for her to take her top off. All I want is to feel the closeness of her smooth skin on mine. I pull at her top and still crying she takes off her cream roll-neck sweater. I touch the smooth material of her white bra and rest my cheek on her chest.

'I can't give you what you need. I can't. Who's going to look after you when I'm gone?'

I get up and kneel on her knee, holding her face in my hands. I wipe away some of Grandma's tears with my thumbs.

'Don't cry Grandma. I love you.'

She looks at me and smiles through her tears. 'My little prince. What would I do without you?'

*

Grandma holds me in her arms as she stands at my bedroom window. We say goodnight to the world together as the birds fly low over the allotments. We pull the curtains closed and then she tucks me into bed.

Later on I walk along the corridor in the dark and open her bedroom door. I creep into her bed beside her where it's warm and cosy. I feel her skin through her nighty and pull the bed covers over my head. I burrow down into the bed and feel for her bare feet. I tickle them, making her laugh and wriggle. I settle behind her back, rubbing her earlobe, and drifting off to sleep.

*

We are leaving Aunty Mary's house in Melbourne. I am sitting in my buggy and Grandma is pulling my hood around my face. She is crying and she has a pretty silk scarf around her hair. She has tears on her cheeks but she is smiling at me. Her face is so, so pretty. She takes a pot of Oil of Ulay out and rubs some first onto her cheeks, and then onto the end of my nose in a fun gesture as she smiles and wrinkles her nose at me.

'What's that cream for Grandma?'

'It protects your skin from the wind and rain.'

We walk on up a long stretch of pavement beside a field to the bus stop. Grandma stops here and looks into the distance, crying again.

'Grandma, why are you crying?'

I can't remember hearing any reply.

We get onto the bus and I play with Grandma's purse, which has a fastener on the top with two metal bulbs protruding up which clasp together making a satisfying click when pushed together.

When we get home, it's just me and Grandma. No dogs. No Granddad. Just us, and Grandma's cough. Grandma puts on a record, and we listen to the haunting sound of 'Johnny, remember me' as we dance around the living room together.

*

Grandma sits at the Singer sewing machine, making it whir and hum as she presses the wrought-iron foot-pedal. She feeds the edge of the trailing curtain into the machine where it is pierced many times by the stabbing needle.

'Make sure you keep your fingers out or they'll get hurt.'

The machine is black and smooth, with a pattern of golden swirls and flowers painted on it. I know why it has 'Singer' written on it; it sings a humming song when Grandma works at it. It is a thing of beauty in my three-year-old eyes, with Grandma sat at it, working the foot-plate up and down, making the wheel at the side go round and round.

*

I am sitting next to Grandma in the Doctor's waiting room. She is reading a magazine with sewing patterns in it, trying not to cough. I look around and everyone looks sad or grumpy. Then Grandma's name is called out and she takes my hand and leads me to a room with a lady in it, and then leaves me sitting on a chair while the lady smiles at me and writes in a book with lines in.

Eventually Grandma returns and takes my hand again. Her face looks sad and worried and she looks like she has been crying. As soon as she gets outside she lights a cigarette under her umbrella. Then we walk home in the rain as I splash my wellies into every puddle we pass.

*

I am outside the house on Martin Street and I am saying goodbye to Grandma on the drive. Grandma is crying and crying. And coughing and gasping for breath. I am leaving with a lady and a man who I know, but I really want to stay with Grandma instead. I have met Mum and Dad before but they are usually the ones that visit and then leave Grandma and I at home. This time they are taking me with them.

Grandma is waving goodbye, standing by the front door with a lady who has her arm around Grandma's shoulders. I go with Mum and Dad. I feel like everything is going backwards, the wrong way. I get into a car and watch Grandma at the door of our house, waving, as we drive away. I look and wave back as long as I can still see her until we turn the corner and Grandma is out of sight.

*

Grandma, you wondered if I would live, if anyone would help me to survive. I did live. I made it. You left me a legacy of stability, security, and self-worth. You helped me to survive. And the God of Heaven heard your prayers in the night and wrapped me in His cloak. He carried me on His shoulders. His hands held me with the strength which you had hoped for. He alone will speak the last, eternal word in my life. The one who lives has led me into His family and I am now His prince, as well as yours.

# 4

# MY FINGERS IN YOUR HAIR

'He was a good boy, who has seen much tragedy.'

Deputy Head Mistress, Firs Estate Infants School.

*

I woke up in bed between two grown-ups. One was Mum, and the other was Dad. Maybe this was what life was going to be like from now on, living with strangers and feeling lost and alone.

Although I hardly knew them, there was something nice about waking up between two people, instead of beside one. I hadn't a clue where I was. I wanted to look out of the small window covered by the wicker blind just to see if I could spot anything familiar.

'Where are we?'

'It's too early. Go back to sleep for a bit,' said Mum as she pulled the sheets over her spring of dark curly hair. I caught a glimpse of her long-lashed green eyes as she rolled away from me.

Dad was lying on his back staring at the ceiling.

'It's my flat, where Mummy and Daddy live,' he said as he turned and smiled at me. He had a strong, craggy face crowned by a mop of black and silver hair. He looked a bit like Michael Parkinson. He lit a cigarette and the room filled with smoke as he puffed away. This was my first morning with Mary and Ted, nestled between the two of them on their soft bed, in their tiny bedroom.

I have no memory of a funeral, or a grave, or anything else to do with Grandma's death. There may have been a period when we lived in the flat while Grandma slipped away at home, or in hospital, but it couldn't have been for long as I have hardly any memories of it. There is a half memory of a visit to a hospital to see Grandma, but it's not full enough to rely upon. When we moved back into Martin Street, Grandma was gone, and it felt like strangers were moving into my home. It would have been even stranger for Mum, who was now moving back into her childhood home, without her mother or father, and with a child she hardly knew. I understood that the house now belonged to Mum and that Grandma had left me some money in a trust fund. 'Three and a half thousand pounds,' the man in the suit told me.

'Your mother and father will look after this for you. You will be able to withdraw it when you are eighteen years old, when you are a grown-up.'

The thought of Grandma leaving money that I would be able to have in the future filled me with even more love and awe for her than I already had.

It also somehow gave her a place in my future. Through part of her will, her desire to go on influencing my life would be fulfilled. A small part of my loss dissolved. She was still there, in my future. But most of my grief remained. Eighteen was a far off, grown-up number.

One evening Mum sat me down at a table and gave me a pen and a piece of paper.

'You can write a letter to Grandma. I'm going to do one too and we can put it in the same envelope.'

'Where is she?'

'She's in heaven.'

'Will she be able to read it in heaven?'

'Yes.'

I sat at the table and spoke my letter to Grandma as I wrote lines and lines of feigned joined-up writing, pouring it out in waves of undulating, slanted lines looped together along the bottom edge.

'Dear Grandma in heaven, I miss you. I love you and I'm sorry that you died. Even though I can't see you I give you a big kiss and a hug. Me and Mummy miss you and I can't wait to see you again one day in heaven.'

As I wrote, I kept looking up through the ceiling into heaven and imagining my grandma looking down on me and smiling. It was a painful thing to do at first because I didn't really want to think about Grandma because I felt so empty when I did. Once I had started, I couldn't imagine why I had not thought about her this much before. When Mum read the letter, and I told her what it said, she cried onto it, smudging the ink of my loopy lines.

There was someone else in the house while Mum and I wrote our letters, helping us, guiding us through. It was a lady but I do not know who she was. She could have been a neighbour, or a teacher maybe. Perhaps she was the same lady who had hugged Grandma on the doorstep as we had driven away. When we had both finished our letters, we put them in the same envelope. Mum wrote 'To Grandma in Heaven' on the front for me, and I put a row of kisses underneath.

*

Dad liked to watch football and wrestling on a Saturday afternoon and he would fall asleep in the chair when the football results were being read out. I used to love watching the men, dressed in leotard-like wrestling suits with braces and shoulder straps. Football was harder to understand but I liked the chanting of the fans and the way the sound brought the atmosphere of the match through the telly into our living room for Dad and I to feel together.

Sometimes he would take me on jobs in his taxi. Dad's taxi was a wonderful place to be. It smelt of amber which seeped from the traffic-light air-freshener dangling from his rear-view mirror. When I was allowed to sit in the front I helped him count his money into a plastic money-rack fixed to his dashboard. Voices would drift into the car from his radio mike and every now and again he would let me press the big button on the side and say something into it like, 'We're just coming back now.' Dad sung along to songs on the radio like, 'Don't cry for me Argentina' and, 'Well hello, Dolly. Feeling swell, Dolly'.

He took me to Chesterfield once and pointed out the crooked church tower. He said it was like that because of woodworms eating away at the beams inside. He drove me along misty country lanes early in the morning where we would stop at farm cafés and eat fried breakfast together in the steamy rooms. We went to London at least once; I remember Dad stopping and pointing up to Big Ben. When in the front, I would sit up and wear my seatbelt, but when in the rear I was allowed to lie down on my back and watch the upside-down sky swoosh by overhead.

I only ever had one conversation with Dad about his other family.

'You've got two older half-brothers and an older half-sister,' he said.

'Where are they?'

'Your brothers are all grown up. They're in the navy now.'

'Are they on a ship?'

'Yes.'

'Has the ship got guns on it?'

'Yes, probably.'

'Do they wear uniforms?'

'Yes, blue ones with white collars.'

'With hats as well?'

'Yes, hats as well.'

'What about my sister?'

'She works as a secretary. She's still living at home with her mum.'

'Who's her mum?'

'That's my wife.'

'I thought you were married to Mummy?'

'Well, I'm not with my wife anymore, I'm with you and Mummy now. I am sort of married to Mummy.'

'Will I ever see my brothers and sister?'

'Yes, probably, one day. Maybe.'

On occasion Dad would drive Mum and I in his taxi to see Aunty Mary in Melbourne. The visits were often laced with tension so I didn't enjoy them that much. The worst bit was when I had to go and see Aunt Allat down the street from Aunty Mary. She was a lovely old lady, with droopy jowls and spectacles on the end of her nose. She would insist on kissing me when we were leaving, which was the bit I never, ever liked. Her kisses always left my cheek wet and I was banned from wiping it off until we were out of sight. 'It's rude to wipe peoples' kisses off,' Mum would say. I didn't care if it was rude. I just wanted Aunt Allat's saliva off my cheek. Aunt Allat always gave me money and always told me not to spend it on sweets.

The journeys back at night were the best bit. I would lie in the back of the car watching the moon follow us through the clouds. We would pour through the racing bends as I swayed from side to side over a bridge, then a gentle hump that left my tummy in the air, and then under a metal pedestrian crossing that straddles the junction. Sometimes we would stop here and Mum would nip out and buy some fish and chips. Then we would go on into the street lights of Derby, around the roundabout with the triangle church, and past the houses. The moon would follow us all the way home from behind the upside-down pointed roofs.

Mum and Dad did argue sometimes but not a lot. When they did, it seemed pretty major. There is one particular time I remember Dad really shouting at Mum and Mum getting really upset. Dad stormed out of their bedroom looking cross and shouting something back at Mum. I watched him disappear down the steps and then went in to find Mum lying on the bed with her face in her hands, crying. She looked up and turned her panda face towards me. All of her mascara had dissolved in her tears and had run down her cheeks. I lay on the soft double bed next to Mum.

'He doesn't even think I'm pretty...'

'I think you're pretty Mum.'

'Thank you darling'.'

Mum started to cry again.

'Why was Daddy shouting at you?'

'He doesn't like my hair. He wants me to wear a wig. A wig...'

Mum started sobbing again. I sidled up closer and put my two fingers into Mum's almost afro fuzz of tightly curled, dark brown hair. My fingers moved, stepped along like an explorer in a jungle.

'My fingers are walking through your *deeeep deeeep* hair.'

Mum laughed, and asked me to do it again. I did, smiling at her.

'Mmmm, that feels so tickly.' Mum was suddenly happy again.

'Do it to my hair Mummy, so I can see what it feels like.'

We did eventually make it out that night and my fingers did the walking from the back of Dad's taxi all the way to the hall where the Big Band were playing. Dad had made it up with Mum, who had combed out her hair into a massive springy afro, defiantly different from all the other ladies there that night. Her green eyes flashed like jewels in the dark rings of her reapplied mascara.

The first thing I noticed about the hall was the tall arched windows at the sides. There were lots of people sitting at huge round tables, drinking beer and wine and eating crisps. The Big Band played away over on the stage with trumpets, trombones, a piano and tapping and snaring drums. Tsk tsk tssss, tsk tsk tssss. Children dodged and weaved between the tables, chasing each other. Dad sat Mum down and went to get some drinks from the bar. My evening was filled with the sounds of the Big Band and the taste of lemonade and cheese and onion crisps. Mum danced away with Dad underneath the glitter-ball with the other grown-ups. By the time the band played 'All do the Hokey-Cokey' I was full of sugar and ready to go. I put my left knee in and my left knee out, all the time grinning from ear to ear at Mum and Dad, who were both holding my hands. During the rush to the middle of the big circle I was whisked off my feet into the air by them both, with adrenaline pumping through a child-sized heart exploding with elation.

The moon was bright on the way back that night, even shining through the wispy clouds. But underneath Mum's springy afro, clouds of confusion were beginning to gather in her troubled mind.

# 5

# SAVE ALL YOUR KISSES FOR ME

'Miss White has a stable relationship with Mr Burrows, who is many years her senior. Mother telephoned on 20th May 1976 saying that she could no longer cope with Dominic. This was unknown to Mr Burrows. It became clear that Miss White was psychiatrically ill and she was admitted to Kingsway Hospital in Derby as a voluntary patient.'

Derby Social Services, 20th May 1976.

*

The strain of looking after a grieving child, when Mum was herself trying to process her own grief – both recent and distant – began to show. Mum had locked me in my bedroom and then called Social Services. Dad was probably out on a job somewhere in his taxi, while Mum was losing the plot at home. I was subsequently received into care for the first time and was taken away to a community home called Elmhurst, while Mum was admitted to Kingsway Psychiatric Hospital.

Although Dad was unable to look after me while Mum was receiving treatment, he visited me every day according to my records. Apparently my admittance to care had been 'extremely traumatic' and I had 'coped very well for a five year old'. The truth is I have hardly any memories of that first time I went into care. I remember being alone in my room for a long time before Mum was admitted. I had a box of Matchbox die-cast metal cars and I remember rummaging in it, looking for my favourites. I also remember weeing into an empty tick-tack box and closing the lid, spilling it all over my hands. I hid the tick-tack box, full of cloudy urine, under the cars at the bottom of my box.

I only have one memory from my three week stay at Elmhurst Children's Home. It was early in the morning and an Afro-Caribbean lady was smiling at me, doing up the togs of my duffel coat. We had been singing, 'Here we go round the mulberry bush, brush our teeth, comb our hair'. We walked down the tree-lined street together hand-in-hand through the morning mist. The trees were dark and tall and had been cut back to knobbly stumps with thin, bare branches of new growth now protruding. Everything was cold and wet and the way ahead was shrouded in a veil of drizzle.

*

I don't remember ever going on holiday anywhere with Mum and Dad but I do remember going swimming with Mum. Queen Street Baths was a warm, humid place and after Mum and my return home in June 1976, we spent many summer days swimming together. This was the time when I began to become close to Mum. Swimming, especially when you are a child learning how to swim with a parent, involves lots and lots of skin–on–skin contact. I was amazed in the changing cubical to see Mum's white skin with its green-snake tattoo. She looked so pretty in the water with her dark curly hair trailing into thousands of drips. This is when I first remember discovering the comfort of Mum's skin. I would guess that whilst Grandma had been very tactile and touchy-feely, Mum had not. I can count all the times I remember Mum hugging me on two hands and most of those times were as an adult. But swimming, well, we couldn't escape each other in the water.

There were windows in the roof of Queen Street Baths which used to allow the sunlight to stream down in shafts and sparkle on the warm water. It felt like a tropical greenhouse with a lagoon in it. Mum would swim lengths in her brown string swimsuit while I held onto the side my armbands on. Then she would take me in her arms and instruct me how to swim. Mum was a strong swimmer and her confidence soon rubbed off on me. I can picture her forearms in the water with the pale strips of flesh where her old tattoos had been surgically removed. She would sneakily let air out of my armbands bit by bit until one day she said, 'Take your armbands off.'

'But I'll sink if I do.'

'No you won't,' she said.

'Yes I will.'

Suddenly I wanted to have my arms on the side of the pool, on solid ground.

'Try it. They haven't got any air in anyway.'

I felt tricked, betrayed. I got over the shock when I slowly realised the implications. Off went the armbands and I was back in love with Mum who had successfully taught me how to swim. For many years after I would tell people, especially people who took me swimming, that my Mum had taught me how to swim with the no-air-in-the-armbands trick. In my opinion this was an awesome legacy – albeit a sneaky one. After that the water became our playground. I would jump in off the lowest springboard as she watched me. She would swim at me underwater from nowhere and I would giggle and splash, skin-on-skin. If anyone ever asks me if I think that skin-on-skin contact can strengthen the maternal bond between mother and child, even a five-year-old child, I tell them that it can and it did.

*

Just after Christmas 1976, when I was five-years old, Dad left home. The Christmas before had been amazing. It was my first Christmas with Mum and Dad. They both went into the back garden and Mum told me to keep a look out with her for Santa. She danced around in the garden, waving at me and pointing up to the sky. I peered out, looking for a sleigh. When I turned around, there on the carpet was a huge pile of presents – Lego, stickle-bricks and a space suit. I had already decided I wanted to become an astronaut when I was older. I put the white suit on and the huge plastic helmet. When the visor came down I could hear myself breathing and feel the warmth of my own breath.

The Christmas just before Dad completely left was different. I sat on the sofa with Mum, who presented me with a box of fuzzy-felt, with shapes to make an air-balloon, people and animals. Dad was not there. Mum had lots of friends around who I didn't know and I played with my Lego amidst a forest of grown-up legs. I built a huge spaceship with spanning wings complete with turrets and ray-guns. I showed my ship to anyone who cared to pay attention, complete with accompanying blaster sound effects.

According to my Social Worker, Dad was older than Mum's dad would have been if he were alive, and was a stabilising influence on Mum. Ted apparently lived a 'conforming' lifestyle, which after five years 'proved too much for Mary to cope with'. In January 1977 Ted approached Social Services in Derby and asked for help with his domestic life. He was extremely emotional and stated that there would have to be a clean break from Mary which would mean that I would lose his support and affection. Ted said that Mary was bringing new boyfriends into the home and was using him as a convenient babysitter.

One day, Mum and I arrived home together to

find a letter on the table. Mum picked up the letter and opened it fast, her breathing getting louder. She read it and sat down, hurt and anger spreading over her features. Tears welled in her eyes as she looked at me.

'Your dad's left us. He's gone back to his wife.'

I suddenly wanted Dad with all my being.

'I want Daddy. I want to see Daddy. Can we phone Daddy and tell him to come back?'

'He said that he doesn't want to see us anymore. It's over between me and your Dad.' Mum was crying now. 'He says that he loves you but that he can't see you anymore otherwise his wife won't have him back.'

It was so sudden and final, and in a letter! Mum said that he had abandoned us, that he had abandoned me. A desperate pang began to grow inside of me. I wanted to fill the gap back up with Dad's love. I wanted a last word or hug or wink from him, but there was nothing. I could not believe that Dad had suddenly been ripped away, right out of my boyish reach.

'Why can't we phone him? Why not? I want to speak to him.'

Mum still had her leather jacket on. She smelled of fresh air and white musk as she tried to console me. Dad had gone and Mum was becoming distant.

There were some songs that in 1976 captivated me, especially when Mum sang them to me. Dad used to sing 'Combine Harvester' a lot by The Worzels, but Mum picked up a theme tune of the time sung by Brotherhood of Man, as her bitter-sweet love song to me. It was addressed to a three-year old child and explained the stark reality of parental departure and the surety of the hurt which would naturally follow.

Save all your kisses for me.

6

# 'I AM YOUR SISTER'

'Received into care due to mother's inability to cope. Co-hab left three weeks ago. Mother has never cared for child alone. Mother has a history of mental illness. Today tolerance taxed too far (child undemanding). Attempted to strangle Dominic – really a cry for help. Mother concerned for child's well-being but makes unrealistic demands on behaviour and response of a six year old – expects adult reaction to justify small errors. Request for Dominic to be received into care.'

Derby Social Services, 27th March 1977.

*

1977 was not my best year. Mum gave up her job at the staff canteen at British Rail and began to receive supplementary benefit in February 1977. This was to be a year of profound change for Mum and according to my records professionals began to note that she was reverting back to her former lifestyle. She was becoming increasingly disturbed.

There were people, mostly men, coming and going in the house all of the time. There were a couple of men that I really didn't like and who used to babysit me. One was a lodger, who used to sleep in the same bed as me when he babysat. Mum had a showdown with him eventually. I remember sitting in the living room in the morning with Mum, waiting for him to appear through the door from upstairs. Eventually he did.

'Get your things and leave,' Mum snarled at him.

'Why? What have I done?'

I hated the sight of him. He had lank hair and blackheads all over his face. Mum used to say to me, 'If you don't wash your face you'll end up like Ian the lodger.' He shot a look at me as he passed, holding his bag, and left. I was safe, in that moment at least, next to Mum.

At night I used to wake up screaming from a sinister recurring dream. I would be in a playground with other children and the malevolent puppet-like figure of a man would stalk me through the children, hovering, looking for me. Then it would switch to a picture-box spinning around and opening to eerie music, just like on the children's TV programme. Then I would be falling fast and would wake up bolt upright screaming, feeling that I had just landed in my bed from a great height. A fading shadow of the puppet man still dangled above me as the dream slithered away.

I felt like everything was collapsing around me. In the mornings, I would wake up in my room and walk down the long corridor to Mum's bedroom door, which was always locked shut. This used to be

Grandma's door, open to me all the time. Love was just a push of a door away, but now I knocked, rattled the handle, and banged.

'Mum. Mum. Muuuum? Can I watch telly?'

Mum shouted at me from behind the locked door.

'Go back to bed.'

'But can I watch telly? I want to watch telly. Can you come and switch the telly on? Mum, I want to watch telly.'

'I said, go back to bed. Play in your room for a while. It's too early.'

I would go back and play. After a while I would walk back down the long corridor to Mum's white, closed door.

'Mum, it's not early any more. Can I watch telly now? Can I?'

Eventually Mum would thunder out and grab hold of my arm and drag me back to my bedroom, putting me firmly back to bed.

One morning the drama of seeking and denying attention progressed beyond the arena of the corridor. Our stairs in Martin Street were at the side of the house behind the living room and were enclosed behind a door which opened out into the corner of the living room.

The conversation started in the living room. I was upset and I was pushing the long plastic buttons at the side of the blank television screen.

'I want to watch telly.'

'I want to watch telly.'

'I want my grandma.'

'I want my grandma.'

Mum turned towards me and spat out her gut-wrenching revelation.

'She's not your grandma. She's your mum. She was your mum. I'm your sister.' Mum was breathing hard through her nose. She smirked when I started to wail. 'Yeah, I'm your sister. Your grandma was your Mum as well as mine. She was too embarrassed to tell all her friends that she'd had another baby when she was so old. She lied and told everyone that I was your mum. But I'm not.'

Mum's attack was convincing. I had just enough doubt in my mind to begin believing that it was true. Suddenly I didn't even have a mum. Only a spiteful older sister who seemed to enjoy seeing me upset.

'I hate you! I hate you!' I cried as I made a run for the stair door and dashed onto the stairs. Mum followed me in a rage. As I sat on the stairs Mum towered over me and pushed me back. It was just me and her in the dark, enclosed space. She grasped my neck and shook and squeezed. I felt her thumbs pressing into my throat and my cheeks went hot. I swayed backwards, and forwards with her. She had a crazed, desperate look on her face; her lips were pulled back tight over her teeth.

'I've had enough of you. I've had enough of you, you little swine.'

I must have passed out. When I came round Mum was gone and I was alone in the dark on the carpeted stairs.

Later on, when I journeyed back into this memory

as an adult it became happily corrupted. Every time I think of it now I imagine Mum as Darth Vader, towering over me. She has her hands around my neck and my tongue is protruding in cartoon fashion. She breathes mechanically and states 'I AM your sister'. Thanks George Lucas; it's much better than the original scene.

Mum called her GP, worried that she might have hurt me. When Dr Tuckley from Harrington Street arrived he put his leather bag down and looked me over from behind his spectacles. He gently lifted my chin with his cold fingers.

'Yes, there is slight bruising but he is more shocked than injured. But the thing is, the child has chicken pox.'

The duty team at Social Services were called and Mum told them that she could not look after me. On 27th March 1977 I was received into care for a second time, feeling very confused and poorly. Because of the chicken pox, I went straight to Ward 4 of Derwent Children's Hospital. There was no drama about going to hospital. It made sense because I had chicken pox. I didn't realise then that hospitalisation for chicken pox was a slightly extreme measure. Few words were exchanged between Mum and I as I left with the Social Worker. The Doctor stayed with Mum.

Even though she had tried to strangle me, I missed Mum whilst I was in hospital. I drew pictures first on paper towels and then on big sheets of white computer paper with perforated edges. I drew dinosaurs being attacked by flying saucers with ray-guns, and cave men throwing spears at the dinosaurs. All these pictures were for Mum, imitations of her drawings that she would sometimes do for me.

The nurses at the hospital were all kind and could all have been my Mum, or my grandma. I was a dry sponge soaking up every available scrap of tenderness or kindness on offer. From the moment I arrived I got so much sympathy and attention. Smiling ladies fed me jelly and ice cream and plumped my pillows. I got out of bed and helped them to pull my bottom sheets tight and tuck the corners neatly under the mattress. My sheets were smooth and cool but my sores itched and itched.

'Do not scratch your spots young man, or pick the scabs off,' the nurses would tell me. 'If I find any scabs in your bed you'll be in trouble.'

'I can't help it. They itch so much.'

'If you scratch off your scabs you'll get infected and it will make scars.'

'Scars?'

'Yes, scars – horrible, pale scars all over your legs and tummy.'

'I don't want scars.'

'Well stop scratching them then or I'll have to put mittens on you.'

I remember the mittens. They were the most annoying things and I felt punished and silly with them on my hands. It was a sign to all – kind nurses, curt doctors and even other patient's relatives – that

I was a failure and couldn't be trusted not to scratch my scabs.

Bath times were unusual at Derwent Children's hospital, for people with chicken pox at least. The bath was in the middle of a small, square room with lifting apparatus dangling over it. The water was cool and laden with a milky substance called chamomile. It smelt funny and medical. I would be left alone in the room for what seemed like hours, sitting in the big bath as the water got colder and colder. Eventually I shouted for help.

'I'm ready now. I've finished. I've had my bath now... I'm ready!'

More than ready.

Nights were the worst part of being in hospital. All I wanted to do was go to sleep and stay asleep. There were so many lights and beeping noises and people talking. And the nurses kept waking me up and making me take medicine. The worst night was when the girl with whooping cough came in. She was in the bed next to me, with the curtains pulled around. Each long whooping breath was fought for agonisingly by the little girl, followed by a torrent of coughs and splutters. This went on and on, as people milled around behind the curtain.

'Whoooooooop..... Crackle, crackle crackle.'

'Whoooooooop..... Crackle, crackle, crackle, crackle crackle.'

As I lay awake in bed I felt so sorry for the girl. I wished I could take it away and help her to breathe. Hearing someone else struggle for breath is one of the hardest things. It reminded me of Grandma's coughing fits. Of course, it's much harder if you are the one fighting for breath. That night was long and mostly sleepless.

Eventually I was moved to a room with a door and walls rather than a curtain. This was not a positive development for me because I was left alone for long periods of time and I missed the nurses. My social worker paid me a visit, wearing a face mask, an apron and some white gloves. I felt infectious and isolated. She told me that I was being isolated because of my chicken pox. She was nice enough though. It was pleasant to see someone who I had met before outside of the hospital.

'Dominic, I am going to be your social worker from now on. I am going to be working to help you and your mum.'

Having a social worker, 'my' social worker, was a difficult concept for me to grasp. This was the lady who had showed up at our house when things weren't great and she was the lady in whose car I would be driven away. But now she was going to be 'my' social worker. I liked Mrs Brown and was glad that she was mine but I wanted her to take her gloves off, and her mask.

The last days in Derwent Children's Hospital were lonely. Nurses would sometimes come in to bring me food, or change my bedding, but most of the hours were spent alone looking out of the window. At least it was easier to sleep at night.

On 7th April 1977 I was returned home to Mum at

Martin Street, despite the plan being for me to be again received into care and taken to a children's home. My records say that Mum 'asked for the child's return home'. Mum had recovered and was ready to recover me.

Again.

# 7

# WHO LOVES YA, BABY?

It was my sixth birthday on April 23rd 1977 and I was out of hospital and at home at Martin Street. Lots of my school friends were invited and it was to be a fancy-dress party. There had been much talk of it in the playground at Firs Estate Infant School.

'What you coming as Gary?'

'Superman! He can fly and I've got his cape.'

'What you coming as Darren?'

'I'm Spider-Man. Or a pirate. Or Batman.'

'Which one are you then?'

'Spider-Man. What about you Dom, what you going as?'

'I don't know yet. It might be Batman or something like that.'

'Eh? It's your own party and you dunner even know what you're going as?'

'No, not yet.'

'Why don't you know yet?'

'I haven't decided. Mum said she'd make me a costume anyway.'

*

When I got home, Mum handed me a black,

fuzzy wig, and a pair of tights. I looked up at her with a sinking feeling in my tummy. Mum was happy and went on to try and sell her idea.

'You can go as someone from *Planet of the Apes*. You like them don't you?'

I liked *Star Trek*, and *Champion the Wonder Horse*, and *The Lone Ranger*, and *Thunderbirds*, and *Black Beauty*. I used to love the theme tune to *Black Beauty*. I liked *Wurzel Gummage*, and *Buck Rogers*, and *The Tomorrow People*, and *Doctor Who*. There were so many much better telly programs than *Planet of the Apes*. But Mum liked *Planet of the Apes*. I looked at Mum's excuse for a good costume as she held it out to me.

'Girls wear tights. Everyone will laugh at me.'

'No they won't. They'll all be having too much fun to notice what you're wearing.'

'They won't know that I'm from *Planet of the Apes*. They'll think I'm dressed up as a girl.'

'No they won't. You'll see. Try them on and see how it looks. At least you've got an outfit. Some children don't even have any outfits to wear at fancy dress parties.'

I put the tights on and felt naked. Mum did something to them round the back to make them stay up. The wig was itchy and too big. It kept falling off or slipping over my face. When it was on it made me hot and sweaty.

As the time approached for everyone to arrive, I became nervous and wondered if anyone would turn up. I was surprised when people did – first a few and then loads: superheroes, fairy princesses and a few pirates. Every person I greeted, children and grown-ups alike, got a delivery of my explanation.

'I'm an ape from *Planet of the Apes* on telly.' I still felt naked in the tights.

'Yes, you are aren't you? Very good,' strained the grown-ups.

I received little attention or comment from my school friends. They were more interested in playing out who they had come as, or just playing in general. One boy took the time to ask me, 'Where's your gun then?'

There was a big table with sandwiches, jelly and cake on it, and I sat at the top. I ate and ate. When the table had been moved to the side everybody jumped around and climbed on the sofa. We were all hyper, full of sugar and pop. I can't remember any party games. As people started to leave there was some tension between Mum and some of the grown-ups who were coming to collect their children. People cleared out fairly quickly and left Mum and I alone to clear up the mess. There was cake and jelly everywhere, trodden into the carpet. Mum shot a few sharp words at me because I had embarrassed her in front of her friends but I had no clue what I had done. Off came the wig and the tights, which was a great relief. Now I was six.

*

In the morning someone knocked on the door early and woke Mum and I up. The parcel was for me and it had been delivered by a charity that helps mums and children. It was a charity birthday present. I think Mum bought me a scooter for my 6th birthday, which I fell off going down the street, gashing my knee. I had an eye-shaped scar for years which lasted much longer than the small round scars on my legs and tummy from scratching off chicken pox.

'Go on then, open it up and see what's inside.'

I pulled the Sellotape back and prised open the lid of the box. I reached inside.

'A doctor's stethoscope! A nurse's hat? A nurse's uniform? Mum, I think they've sent a girl's one by accident. It's a nurse, not a doctor.'

'Aw, never mind. Try it on and see how it looks.'

'Mum, it's a nurse's outfit for girls to wear. I don't want to be a nurse.'

'Go on, put it on.'

As I pulled it free from the box a lollipop fell from the folds onto the floor.

'And a lollipop Mum.'

On went the uniform. It was a dress with a plastic upside-down fob watch attached to the breast pocket. I put the stethoscope around my neck and positioned the hat. I knew it was a girl's nurse's outfit but it felt much better than just a pair of tights. Mum looked at me and smiled.

'You look great. Put the lollipop in. Can you say "who loves you baby'?'

This was Kojak's famous catchphrase. Kojak was a bald, American detective we used to watch on TV. I unwrapped the sugar lollipop and shoved it in my mouth and grinned.

'Wholovesya baby?'

Mum was in hysterics.

'Why don't you go round to Darren's house and show him and his mum your impression of Kojak in a nurse's outfit?'

So off I went down the street and round the corner with my stethoscope, fob watch, nurse's outfit and my lollipop, to Darren's house. I practised as I walked down the street in the sunshine, trying not to crunch my lolly.

'Wholovesya baby?'

'Wholovesya baby?'

Kojak asked women that question but I was starting to ask myself. I wanted to ask it to ladies, like Kojak did. If only I could be back in hospital now, with my cute catchphrase, and my outfit. But the question became heavier.

'Wholovesya baby?'

'Who loves ya baby?'

'Who loves you baby?'

'Who loves *you* baby?'

By the time I got round to Darren's house I had run out of steam and my delivery lacked conviction. Darren's mum looked like Wonder Woman when she was in disguise. She wore huge round glasses and a big smile. She laughed at my joke and gave me a hug. It felt weird getting a hug when I was wearing a dress. Darren laughed at the outfit rather than the catchphrase, but soon forgot about my dress and played with me regardless.

On the way back I said the line in my head over and over. I liked Kojak so much, and the Streets of San Francisco, and Hawaii 5-O, and Starsky and Hutch. They were all telly programmes I used to watch with Dad. Dad understood them and laughed at the jokes. I laughed because he laughed. Even now, if I hear any of those theme tunes, it takes me back to Martin Street to Dad – to sitting on his knee and watching American cop dramas with him.

That night I lay in bed awake for a while, listening to the cars slide by in the rain. Every time one passed, the headlights would trace a path across the ceiling as the light shone through the gap between the top of the curtains and the wall. I had two windows in my bedroom at the front corner of the house so I got the light show twice for free. The sound of every car reminded me of Dad's taxi.

On my sixth birthday, and the days following, I really missed my Dad. But as it happened, it would not be too long before I saw him again.

# 8

# FATTY MEAT AND BOILED POTATOES

- Date admitted to care: 28.04 1977
- Relevant Act: Section 1: 1948 Act
- Reception to: Community home
- Status: Illegitimate
- Address from which child admitted: 142 Martin Street, Derby
- Reason for care: Increased behaviour disturbance in the child. Father left the home January 1977. Request by mother for voluntary care. She is unable to cope with the situation
- School: Firs Estate Infants
- Achievements and social relations at school: Bright child, who has become withdrawn in class
- Connection with Church: St Wurburg's Church
- Known desirable/undesirable friends: Mother's friend – Andy Roe/Bridgett
- Present health and habits: Eats well, dislikes fatty meat and potatoes. Has been waking at night. He is scared of going to bed. * Night time enuresis
- Any previous separations/illnesses etc? Admitted to care 20.05.1976. Mother in hospital. Request for care 27.03.1977. Admitted to hospital with chicken pox. Father – Returned to wife in Littleover, Derby. Earnings – Not known. States not

father of child.

- Attitudes / opinions about child above: Mother tries to cope with child. I considered that she was creating child tantrums. Various men friends in the house. Dominic left with male babysitter, who has been taking child out and sleeping with Dominic. Dominic has a strong dislike of this man. Mother unstable. Burrows is now denying paternity.

Derby Social Services, 28th April 1977.

*

Mum started to call me 'Dougie' around this time, and dress me in dungarees with a blue patch of a thumb on the front pocket which said 'keep on truckin'. I felt strange in dungarees as I had never seen anyone else wearing them.

'Dungarees are cool Dougie, they look great on you. Keep on truckin' Dougie.'

Sometimes Mum would call me 'Dougle', a slight variant on Dougie. Mum loved The Magic Roundabout telly programme with the floppy dog with no legs called Dougal. Mum told me that Zebedee, who jumped around on a spring, was 'on speed', and that Ermintrude the dopey cow smoked 'de herb'. Mum liked The Magic Roundabout a lot more than I did. I knew about the herb or dope. Sometimes when we went out to places, I would have to carry packages of it wrapped in cling-film in my pants. If the police asked me if I had anything in my pockets, or in my pants, I was always supposed to say no. Dope was so lumpy and it rubbed my legs when I walked.

Mum started to move the furniture around as well, usually when I was trying to watch the Star Trek cartoon on the telly. Mum would be hoovering and moving, and the telly would get unplugged and moved to the other side of the room just when the aliens were coming on. During the week, I would often get home after school to find a new arrangement to get used to – new name, new dungarees, new seating arrangements, but the same old babysitters. There was one man who I tried to refuse to be left with. He had a fingertip missing and said that he had accidentally put his finger in the bread-slicing machine at the bread factory at work. He joked that someone would find it in their sandwich soon. I felt sick and unsettled when he was around.

Even at that lowest of times there were still good things to cling on to. Mum had started to go to a church and take me with her. It was a strange place where people fell down and then praised the Lord, but the carpet was soft and I liked the smell of the wooden seats.

Mum got me into plastic model kits around this time as well. She sat with me and helped me to fix and paint two dinosaur Airfix models. One was a triceratops, painted green with brown highlights on its bumps, and the other one was a T-Rex with little arms. I made a few aeroplanes as well and a small battle ship, but Mum wasn't interested in those.

Bath time in the green bathroom was one of my favourite things of all. It would be all hot and steamy, like Queen Street Baths, and Mum would play me her tune on her smooth wooden guitar with an orange sunburst on the front. She always plucked the same three strings with her thumb, hammering the strings onto the fret board with one finger. Then the tune would move down a string, then back up. Always the same tune, which she eventually taught me how to play.

'It's a Red Indian tune. The Braves play it to the Squaws at night in their Teepees.'

If she wasn't strumming her guitar she was singing pop songs and shaking her maracas, or scraping the stick along the oval thing with lots of wooden ridges on it. Mum would sing Bob Dylan songs and 'Blinded by the light.' I liked Mum's taste in music then. She would stand and iron in the living room, listening to 'Fifty ways to leave your lover,' and 'Are you going to Scarborough fair?' My favourite record she used to play was an old one called 'Johnny, remember me'. It reminded me of Grandma, because she used to play it too. It was a haunting record, with a drumbeat like horses' hooves galloping.

The saddest song Mum used to listen to was 'Mr Bojangles'. She would sing along with it, tossing her head back and letting his name out into the air above her upturned face. The words used to make me sad because it had a dog in it who died, and it reminded me of Grandma's dogs Mick and Megan.

Some nights were fun when people came around and played music and smoked a lot. Mum would draw me spacemen to colour in and I would sit at Grandma's old Singer sewing machine with the machine turned over and sunk into the table making a good flat surface for colouring. I liked looking at the patterns on the machine and trundling the iron foot-pedal. It reminded me of Grandma. Once Mum went out and left me alone. She gave me strict instructions not to open the draws of the sewing machine and play with the needles and bobbins. When Mum had gone, I opened the front draw at the top, and then all three side draws, looking for interesting things. I found scraps of leather which I held and sniffed, leather punches, and ribbons and studs. When I heard the door opening I stuffed all the treasure back into the wrong draws and got into big trouble.

Sometimes at night I cried because I was so tired, but soon I settled back down to colouring in Mum's art work – spacemen in spacesuits and the helmets with the long things at the side with the aerials on. Mum's marker pen squeaked on the white paper as she drew amazing worlds and creatures. They all flowed effortlessly from the tip of her black pen, which smelled so nice when the top was off. Mum's drawing was much better than my matchstick cavemen and lumpy dinosaurs. I wished that I could draw like her.

Constructions in Lego continued through the

night too, mostly elaborate spaceships that fell to pieces when you tried to pick them up. Sometimes I started a house, usually with a grown-up because that's what they seemed to want to build, but I found earth dwellings boring and hardly ever got to building the roof. I had a huge box of Lego, mostly green, white and red bricks with a few black, yellow and blue ones. I remember the feel of it in my hands as I rummaged in the box, and the sound the bricks made as I searched for that special piece.

I had two Action Men. One had brown hair and the other had ginger hair with a beard. Mum would treat me sometimes by taking me into town and buying me a new Action Man suit flat-packed to a piece of cardboard. Dressing them was tricky but Mum helped me. They became divers, sailors, soldiers and Arctic skiers. My Action Men were well loved even when their soft hands split and hung loose at the fingers.

I was spending a lot of time out of the house during the day as well. Often I would walk around the corner at the top of the road and take myself to the park past Darren's house. It was a big green field with trees in it that rose up a hill into the mysterious distance where only dog walkers and couples holding hands dared to go. I stuck to the playground with the slide, swings and wooden roundabout where all the older kids played. It was a happy place for me, apart from one incident which I still to this day find disturbing.

Some older kids were throwing darts from the top

of the slide onto the roundabout below. They were proper darts, with metal spikes at the end of their heavily weighted bodies. Some boys gave me a dart, with union jack flights, and guided me up to the top of the slide.

'Go on! Throw it down onto the roundabout. Quick, go on!'

There were girls on the roundabout, older girls, who were looking up and shouting, 'No, don't listen to them.' followed by laughing.

'Go on then. Don't be a chicken. Try and get it to stick in the wood.'

I could feel his knees pressing into my back and people at the bottom of the slide were shouting for me to hurry up because they wanted a go on the slide. I stood, dart in hand, watching the two girls go round and around. I could see no way out. I focussed on the timing of the spins below, keeping my eyes on the empty triangle sections of brightly painted wood between the metal rails.

Round.

And round.

And round.

And round.

My elbow bent. Then my hand flicked forward and sent the dart gliding. It sailed then plummeted. There was a scream, followed by a wail. My smile melted away as I looked down at the girl holding her leg. Her friend was hugging her shoulders and shouting up at me.

'You stupid idiot. Look what you've done. She's

bleeding now.'

There came a voice from behind. 'Quick, you better run home before the police catch you.'

So I slid and I ran. I looked back to see the girl walking away from the playground, surrounded by other girls. The boys were drifting along at a healthy distance behind. I was the criminal though. I was the one who hit the girl's leg with a dart. Even as I turned and ran on I felt so bad about what I had done. I meant to hit the wood not the girl. I wanted to go back in time and take the shot again, only this time I would get the timing right and hit the wood and miss the girl. I had drawn blood and caused pain. I was the bad one. This was how I began to feel most of the time. Although Mum was trying, she was blaming me a lot when things went wrong.

*

Teatime on April 28th 1977, five days after my birthday, did not work out well. I sat at the table with a plate full of disgusting food that I didn't want to eat. I had tried the meat but quickly spat it back onto the plate. It was chewy and had big lumps of cold gristle and fat on it. The boiled potatoes were big and dry and had bad bits in them. Grandma used to cut the bad bits out and mash the potato up with butter and milk. I was refusing to eat the fatty meat and dry potatoes.

'I don't want it. I'm not hungry anymore.'

'Stop wailing and eat your dinner.'

'I don't want to'.

'Eat your bloody dinner.'

'Naaaaaaaaah, I don't want it any more. Aaaaaaaaaaah.'

'You're not getting down until you've eaten your bloody dinner.'

Mum plonked herself down in the chair beside me and pushed the plate closer to my chest. She sniffed and stared at me.

'There's nothing wrong with it. Eat it.'

'I don't want to.' I said in a quieter voice between rhythmic sobs.

I looked, and waited, wondering what Mum's next move would be. I wanted to be in control of what stuff I did or did not have to put into my mouth, and chew, and swallow. Mum also wanted to be in control of this.

'Is it not up to your royal standards? It's food and there's nothing wrong with it. Eat it or I'll shove it down your throat.'

'No, I don't want it.'

Mum reached for the fork and took a shovel full. My head thrashed from side to side trying to avoid it. Mum flew up and braced my head from behind thrusting a forkful of food into my crying, open mouth. My cheeks suddenly burned and I smashed my fists onto the table. The plate flew to the side and clattered to the floor. Meat and potato exploded over the carpet, followed by the splash of my drink.

Before I knew it I was thrown onto the floor on my knees. Mum was crying now.

'Pick it up. Just pick it up.'

Mum had really lost it now. She was crying and crying, saying 'Pick it up' over and over again through gritted teeth. She was suddenly a wreck and I was scared. I felt as if I had done this to Mum. I was the bad one. What followed next is mostly a blur to me but I remember bits of it.

Mum has gone, and I am crying in the hall. I look through the glass in the door. I can just see Mum pacing on the drive through the thick, dimpled glass. I scream.

'Let me out. Let me out. Let! Me! Out!'

I kick the glass. I kick it again and it cracks.

Then I am standing in the living room holding a broom in my hand. Mum is standing over me, seemingly composed and almost encouraging.

'Go on then, do your worst. Smash it.'

I pull back the broom and swing it at the telly screen. It clunks and bounces off the thick glass. I swing again with more conviction, and it clunks and bounces backwards again. This time the vibration through the wooden pole into my hands hurts.

'Eh, it's not as easy as you think is it?'

I look around for an easier target. I spot the high window that Granddad used to peep through when he came home. I lift the broom aloft and aim for the small square of glass. The broom head smashes straight through and I look back at Mum to see how she will respond.

'There, do you feel better now?'

Then I'm being pushed out of the front door,

which is slammed closed behind me. I cry and scream and bang my fists onto the top pane of dimpled glass. I step back and look at the bottom pane which is cracked. I turn and scan the ground opposite the front door, looking for stones to throw. I get down on my haunches and crawl along the edge of the allotment grass. I find a piece of brick and throw it hard at the top glass like I'm doing a shot-put. The glass cracks. Mum appears behind the cracked glass shouting for me to stop it. I pick the same brick up, go back a short distance, and throw it again. This time the glass crumbles and the brick disappears into the hall.

Then I'm sliding backwards along the outside wall of the house. My jumper is catching on the roughness of the bricks as I retreat. It feels like I am being more dramatic than I actually feel now, like I am putting on a show. I feel like I was that angry but not anymore. I had just unleashed rage and anger by smashing and destroying. I was not about to land without a long runway. The social worker approaches me and puts out her hand. No gloves this time.

'Come on. It's okay. You can come with me.'

I put my hand out and slowly stop the rhythmic heaving I have cried myself into. She holds my hand and we pass Mum as I get into the car. Mum stands and talks to the social worker and then Miss Brown gets into the car and we drive away. We leave Mum and my dinner behind at Martin Street.

# 9

# SILVER JUBILEE

'The house was always full of people. The people, according to Mary, lived off her, which led to financial difficulties. Mary found a baby sitter for Dominic, whom when I met I knew to be a man known to the probation department. He was an extremely disturbed man and he was thought at that time to be schizophrenic.'

'Dominic was at times distraught, he was physically violent. I felt Mary had caused some of the scenes, I felt she was goading Dominic to act out the hostilities. On one occasion when she could not control the situation she went outside the house. Dominic went berserk to be left in the house alone and kicked in the glass door. On talking to the GP I learned that Mary's behaviour was the same as Dominic's when she was his age.'

Miss B S B, Social Worker, Derby Social Services. April 1977.

'Received with bruises – one large unexplained on thigh.'

Derby Social Services, 28th April 1977.

*

It was about much more than food preferences. Leaving the house, and Mum, felt right this time, but it didn't make it any easier.

As soon as I arrived at Porter Road, I knew that I did not want to stay. My Social Worker left me with strangers. The woman, who had a grey bun of hair above her spectacled face, started by telling me off. 'We won't have behaviour like that around here, young man!'

This was a reference to my behaviour at home. She didn't understand me, or she would not have said that.

'You will have to do as you're told as long as you are here with us.'

I looked up at her brown cardigan, but didn't meet her eyes.

'I want Mum.'

'You can't have Mum after your behaviour today.'

'I want to ring Mum.'

'No, you can't. You'll just have to do without.'

I screamed and cried. I jumped on and off the sofa. The lady left. I continued to scream at the top of my lungs.

'I want to ring Mum!'

Eventually the lady returned. Without a word she grabbed me by the arm and marched me to a smaller room and sat me in a chair. On the small table was a telephone.

'Only a quick call.'

She dialled the number, introduced herself and handed me the phone.

I cried. 'I want to come home Mum. I don't like it here. I don't like it.'

'I want you home too my love but I've got to sort myself out first.'

'I'm sorry. I promise not to do it again. Please can I come home?'

'Not now. I will come and see you soon though. Miss Brown said it would be okay.'

'But I want to see you now Mum.'

The phone was taken from me and I started screaming again.

*

On 7th June 1977 there were street parties all over Derby for the Queen's Silver Jubilee. There was such a build up to the celebration at Porter Road Children's Home and at my new school. Red, white and blue bunting was draped across the streets at every turn and there was endless talk about the Queen. I might have enjoyed the build up more if I had not felt so disapproved of and naughty. There was a threat hanging over me; if I didn't behave myself I would have to miss the street party.

By the time the day came it was a total anticlimax. A different lady at Porter Road dressed me in preparation, whilst another one looked on.

'You need to look smart. Here you are. Try this on for size.'

I put the black jacket on over my white shirt. It was a job to get it on and it felt too tight under the arms. The lady bent down and pulled and wrenched at my shirt and the jacket. When she was satisfied, she stepped back and smiled.

'There, that looks smart. The arms are a bit short but it'll do. All you need now is a smart tie to wear.'

'I don't want to wear this jacket. It's too tight.'

The other lady leaned forward and pulled my white shirt cuffs down past the ends of the jacket sleeves. The cuffs stuck out past the ends. It felt a bit better.

'There, that's more like it. You look like a little Chinaman you do.'

They both laughed at me, but I didn't think it was funny. I did not want to wear a jacket, or look like a little Chinaman. I just knew that no-one else would be wearing a jacket. I looked down at the front; it was too long and the arms were way too short.

The lady with the grey bun and glasses just about dragged me through the bunting-clad streets to wherever we were supposed to be. I was receiving a ticking off along the way for something I did or didn't do at school, and I was told in no uncertain terms that I would need to improve. I wanted to kick her and run away but I didn't.

Although I remember being marched along the way, I have no recollection of a street party. Perhaps it was a brief engagement for me. Neither do I remember having the photo taken that I found on the Internet. I recognise some of the children beside me in it, boys and girls from my new school. The little boy sitting next to me had an extra little finger, which he had to have surgically removed. When he came back to school after the operation and we all gathered around him to look, he said that he could still feel it wiggling.

There I am, sitting on the front row grinning with my white sleeves shining in the sun. I am the only one in the photograph, adults included, who is wearing a jacket.

Porter Road wasn't all bad, mind you. I got used to it and just got on with it. I do not remember any other children being there although there almost certainly were. I had a nice bedroom which overlooked lots of back gardens with washing on lines billowing in the breeze. I would watch the light fade through my green curtains and then settle down into my bed under the window.

The best part of being at Porter Road was that my Dad visited me. I had not seen Dad for six months and I had thought that I would never see him again. It was such a strange and emotional surprise when he arrived and ruffled my hair. He took me out in his taxi and we went to cafés and drank banana milkshake.

'Can I come and live with you, Dad?'

'Not at the moment. We'll see. Maybe one day.'

Dad and I went out in his taxi once again. We sang along to sad songs like 'Don't cry for me Argentina, the truth is I never left you. All through my wild days, my mad existence, I kept my promise.

Don't keep your distance.' and 'Dolly don't ever go away again.' They all seemed to be about people going away. But when I was in my Dad's taxi, which was warm and smelled of amber air freshener and Dad's Old Spice after shave, everything was all right with the world.

I saw Mum once whilst I was at Porter Road. It was one of the sunniest, hottest days I remember in Derby. We went to an outdoor swimming pool at Markeaton Park where we met one of my former babysitters. He was a fat man with glasses and lank hair. He had a protruding gut which bulged through his tee-shirt. At one point Mum was trying to leave me with him while she went off to do something or other. He bent down, his face at my level. 'I'll buy you a ninety-nine flake.'

'No, I don't want Mum to go.'

'Don't you want an ice cream then, Dominic?'

'Yes I want one but I want Mummy to buy it.'

I ended up stood in the queue in front of the ice cream van holding his sweaty hand.

I spent most of my time that day sitting underneath the curtain of water that poured from the plinth-shaped fountain in the middle of the paddling pool, sheltering from the heat. I spent as much time as I could inside the fountain, hiding away from Mum's fat, smelly friend. When I eventually emerged and looked for Mum and the babysitter I could not see them anywhere. I ran around through the hordes of people lying down on towels on the grass until I finally spotted Mum sitting back down.

'Where have you been? I've been looking everywhere for you. I thought you had gone and left me Mum.'

'I've been here all the time you daft apath.'

*Oh no you haven't*, I thought.

*

On the way back I asked Mum why I couldn't come home and live with her. I clung on to her hand at the door of Porter Road, not wanting to let go.

'I'm just sorting myself out a bit. You wouldn't want it to be like it was before would you?'

'No.'

That year, 1977, the Queen made the town of Derby into a city. She came to visit Derby for the occasion. I'm not sure that she ever saw me in my ill-fitting jacket under the 'Welcome to Derby' banner but there I was, especially 'poshed up', waiting for her. But really, even the Queen didn't stand a chance of getting much attention from me anyway. The person I wanted most of all was my Mum.

# 10

# JOURNEY IN THE NIGHT

- Date: 30th June 1977.
- Discharge from: 91 Porter Road.
- To: 142 Martin Street, Derby.

'Dominic remained at Porter Road for eight weeks during which time Mary seldom visited. After six weeks he was becoming withdrawn. Ted Burrows visited and took the child out. Then Mary asked for child's return in social worker's absence, and immediately took him to Cornwall and left him with relatives for the duration of the summer holidays.'

*

When I got home, I realised that the house was different. Mum's art had leapt from the poster papers and was now all over the walls and there was a funny smell. Mum had lit a 'joss stick'. There was also a huge black-and-white circle chasing itself around on one wall.

'What's that circle, Mum?'

'It's a yin and yang. It's the balance of the universe. Darkness and light. Good and evil, in perfect harmony.'

There was a picture of a tiger on another wall peering with a beady eye from behind tall, green grass. It looked like he wanted to eat me.

There was also a black cat with green eyes just like Mum's.

'Dougie, we're gonna go and see your Uncle Bob and Aunty Becky in Cornwall.'

The motorbike was a Suzuki 250cc and was parked in the front drive. In the few short days that followed, our front drive became very popular with teenage boys from up the street.

'Mary, gimme another go on yer bike.'

'Don't go off the street and wear the helmet.'

Up and down they went, one after the other, making a terrible racket. At least one parent came and confronted Mum.

'If you give him another go I'm calling the police on yer.'

Mum took pains to make sure that she explained how to handle and operate the bike to the less experienced boys.

'This is the clutch and this is the brake. Make sure you let the clutch out slowly, or you'll fall off backwards.'

Mum would make them show her how they would do it whilst the bike was at a standstill. Teenage girls stood nearby looking on and chattered amongst themselves. I wondered if the girl who had been brutally spiked in the leg by my hopeless dart throw was around.

'This is the revs. Twist it like this.' The engine

spluttered to life as Mum did her demonstrations.

Somehow the bike and the teenagers survived and it was time for Mum and I to hit the road. I watched as Mum strapped the bags to the metal grill at the back of the bike with coloured bungee ropes which had metal hooks on the end. She seemed happy and relaxed as the cat weaved around her boots while she pulled the bungees tight. There were a few bags and a rolled-up bundle of some stuff. The seat of the motorbike was amazing; it seemed so big. There was the bit that Mum sat on and then a raised portion further back where I would be sitting. Mum gave me an especially big lump of dope to put in my pants. By the time the day had cooled and the evening sun was shining onto the windows of the house, we were ready to set off on our adventure, together.

*

'Lean with the bike. If I turn this way, you lean with it. If I turn that way, you do the same. And make sure you hold on. It's easy.'

Excited was not sufficient a word for how I felt. I climbed up onto the back of the Suzuki and pulled my helmet on. Mum helped me to tighten the strap underneath my chin and wiggled the helmet to check it was tight enough.

'Ow! My ears!' I joked.

'That'll do. Are you ready for a holiday, Dougie?'

'Yes Mum. Where is Cornwall? How long will it

take to get there?'

'It's a long way away by the sea. It should take a few hours or so before we get there.'

Mum swung her leg over the smooth green petrol tank and kicked the beast into life. I could feel the vibration of the engine in my legs.

'Hold on tight Dougie.'

'OK Mum.'

I clutched on to Mum's leather jacket as tightly as I possibly could and leant close to her as she kicked the stand away from the ground. Her skin was covered in cow-skin but I was still unusually close. Suddenly the beast was freestanding, balanced by Mum's toes on either side. As I felt the gentle sway for the first time I smiled from ear to ear. I was smiling inside from my feet to my scalp. My tummy rolled as Mum pushed off and away we went into the fading evening light.

Feeling the pull of the engine was exhilarating. If I let my body fall back slightly away from Mum's back, I could feel the gentle tug of the wind on my front. Wearing the helmet with the visor down over my face felt strange at first. As we snaked through the first major corner onto the Burton Road, I quickly learned what 'lean with the bike' did, and didn't mean. Mum turned and I leant down as far as I could, getting closer and closer to the road as the bike leant over to the right. As I leant I thought to myself, this doesn't feel right.

'Pull up, Dougie! Pull up!'

The bike stayed low, and I suddenly realised that

my lean was causing the bike to lean too. I had almost pulled Mum off the bike with me but she managed to hang on. I wrenched on Mum's jacket to straighten myself up as she let out the clutch. The bike suddenly pulled away causing me to sway backwards onto the bags at the back. I almost fell off the back as the bike straightened. Then the front end of the bike lifted up like a rearing horse. I held on with my heart in my mouth as Mum leaned forward to get on top of the handle bars, wrestling the bike back down to the road. We stopped on the pavement. Mum took off her helmet and spun around to face me.

'I said *lean with the bike*, not lean so far we fall off it. You nearly pulled me off.'

My eyes brimmed with tears. 'Sorry Mum.'

Mum's shoulders relaxed and she punched me lightly on the shoulder. 'With the bike – that means you follow me. Keep your back in line with mine and you'll be fine. And keep holding on.'

I smiled. The world was good again.

'Did you see my wheelie?'

'Yeah Mum. Are you supposed to do a wheelie?'

'Not really no, but it was fun. I'm good at it, aren't I? Doing a wheelie?'

'Yes you're good at it, Mum.'

*

The street lights flickered on and the world slipped by underneath our feet as we followed the endless lines of cat's eyes hiding in the middle of the road. I could hear Mum shout back to me every now and again. 'Hold on' or 'Do you need a wee yet?'

It was dark by the time we got onto the big motorway. My eyelids were feeling heavy and the drone of the engine was making me feel sleepy. The road was an endless straight line, leaving me little to do but to fight the drowsiness. I could feel myself leaning backwards more and more as my chin tipped up and the helmet lolled backwards. The bags strapped to the ledge behind me provided a nice backrest, stopping me from lying down on the road behind us. Then it started to rain – a little at first, but then a mesmerising downpour. I could no longer hear what Mum was shouting because of the sound of the rain pattering on my helmet. The water ran in vertical streaks across my visor, blown by the wind as we rushed by.

As we drove on, strange things started to happen. A lorry in front of us kept switching its lights on and off. Then another one did the same. Then cars beeped their horns at us as they passed. I began to feel that everyone was angry with us and that Mum was doing something really wrong.

Suddenly there was more beeping at the side. I saw a car to the right of us, keeping pace with the bike in the driving rain. This was unusual as almost every car had been passing us by, even the beeping ones. The window wound down to reveal a man leaning over from the other side of the car and shouting something at Mum while pointing wildly.

The rain, and the sound of engines, made it hard to hear him.

'Your tail lights! Your tail lights!'

Mum looked back and gave him a thumbs-up. She slowed down and pulled over into the hard shoulder. 'Stay on the bike.'

The bags behind me had worked loose and were hanging over the back of the bike, right over the red lights beneath my seat.

'Look, you've covered up the tail-light. If cars can't see the tail-light they'll run us over. Stop leaning back, will you?'

Mum re-strapped the bags in the rain and we set off again.

Eventually, after hours of rain and darkness, as well as fighting sleep, we arrived somewhere. It was dark and I was wet and tired, and once I had taken off my coat and jeans I collapsed into a warm, soft bed and slept the sleep only people who ride motorbikes through the night can sleep.

My summer adventure in Cornwall had begun.

# 11

# THE BOYS OF SUMMER

At first, I had no idea Mum intended to leave me in Cornwall for the summer. She stayed days rather than weeks but I stayed at least two months. Uncle Bob was Granddad's brother and he had a son whom I called Uncle Kenny, who was Mum's cousin. Granddad's side of the family were from London and Uncle Bob and Uncle Kenny still had their London twangs. The truth is, I can hardly remember Uncle Bob and Aunty Becky but I remember a lot more of my time with Uncle Kenny and his wife Doe.

The day Mum left, we all went to the beach. It was one of those days when the sun was so bright that everything gleamed with colour. The sea came alive with sparkles as the breakers crashed and rolled onto the shingle. I sat in the waves next to Mum, being picked up and rolled backwards. Ahead of me, where the waves rose and crashed down, was a wonder-wall of surf. The waves churned and rolled the pebbles around making a loud gush of watery music.

Mum sat next to me with her same brown swimsuit on that she used to wear in Queen Street Baths. She had dark, round sunshades on under a straw hat. Her skin was oiled with suntan lotion, which I could smell over the freshness of the sea. Everything was big, larger than life, including Mum. She was warm and shiny.

'Do you need some sun-tan lotion rubbing on your back, Mum?'

'Yeah, go on then. Hold your hands out.'

Her skin was warm and soft. I pulled strands of her hair up into her hat so that they were out of the way. Her shoulders were so soft, so Mum. It was so nice being with her when she was happy and when I was happy. I could have stayed in that day, on that beach, forever, whether it was being tossed about in the waves getting salt water up my nose, or lying next to Mum on the warm sand. Even though there were other people around – Kenny and his son Richmond surfing out over the breakers, Doe on a towel and lots of other people on the beach – it was just me and Mum. I had her all to myself. She wasn't going anywhere in that moment; she had no-one else to go off and see. She just lay on the beach next to me.

'When are you coming back to get me Mum?'

She took off her sunshades and looked at me with her green eyes. 'Soon, it won't be long. There's just a few bits and bobs that I need to sort out.'

'When are you leaving?'

'I'll go back to the house and go from there.'

'Can't you stay another day and go tomorrow?'

'No, I've got to go Dougie. If I drive at night it's easier because there's less traffic on the roads. And anyway the cat needs feeding.'

For once I enjoyed being called Dougie – her name for me – even though it wasn't my name.

'How long do you think you might be?'

'I'm not sure, love, maybe a couple of weeks or a bit more. You'll have fun here though. You won't miss me much.'

'Yes I will.'

As we walked up to the top of the beach the sky clouded over and a seagull swooped at me for my ice cream cone. Suddenly the seagulls seemed bigger than me, and threatening too, as they hopped along beside me looking at me with their beady eyes. Uncle Kenny told me not to be scared of them, but I still was.

When we got back to Uncle Kenny's house, Mum packed up her stuff and roared away into the twilight, leaving me behind. I was upset and there was a drama of some sort outside the house. I was trying to get into Uncle Kenny's car so that he could take me back home to Derby. I ended up accidentally trapping someone's fingers in the car door. It could have been my own finger, or Kenny's, or Richmond's. I can't rightly remember.

I think I spent a short time living with Uncle Bob and Aunty Becky at first in Liskeard. I would play in the front garden of their house, rather than the back garden, just so that I could hear Mum's motorbike if she came. I kept asking people when Mum would come back and get me and the answer I got was always 'soon.'

Eventually I moved in with Uncle Kenny, Doe,

Richmond, and Richmond's baby brother Christopher. Richmond was about the same age as me but seemed much older and more sophisticated. He willingly shared his mum and dad with me as well as his bedroom. He got the top bunk and I got the bottom. Richmond was just so cool. He had a wetsuit, a surfboard, and a mum and dad. He would take me a short way across Bodmin Moor to Goldiggings Quarry, which was a disused granite quarry filled up with crystal clear spring water. It was sunken into a green amphitheatre and had stone pillars underneath the water, like some sunken castle. In the deepest parts, the crystal clear water disappeared into the deep blue depths, like an ancient fairy pool.

Bodmin Moor was a good place for an imaginative child to spend time. There were hills, sheep, a circle of standing stones and the towers of disused tin mines scattered around. It was usually misty in the mornings and military aircraft thundered low overhead from time to time. Doe took us for walks on the Moor and to the beach. She took me and Richmond to a farm one day where we took it in turns trying to stay on the back of a huge pink pig. When we weren't abusing the pig by jumping on it, it liked to have its bristly back scratched. Even now, if I see a big pig with bristles on its back, I want to reach out and give it a scratch. I also remember having a big ugly sheep tick on my leg and flicking it's white body repeatedly.

Doe was like a mum to me. She would sit and

read books to me in the garden and tuck me into bed at night. I have visited Kenny and Doe as an adult, who still live in the same old house on the edge of the Moor. It was like walking back into a dream, a pleasant one. There were so many familiar sights to see around the house and across the Moor. In a quiet moment with my wife, when I was out of earshot, Doe's eyes welled up with tears. She told my wife that because she had considered Mary bad news, she felt that she had tarred me with the same brush at the time. She said that she could have been kinder to me and she could have given me a bit more of a chance.

The one and only bad memory I have of my time spent in Kenny and Doe's house was when I threw a tantrum when Mum left. All the rest are warm, bright memories, and seeing Doe again reminded me of how fond I had been of her at the time.

Uncle Kenny was such a great laugh. He was always happy, always had a joke when he was around. I think he must have been away a lot that summer, working hard and 'moving boxes'. At the time I didn't have a clue what he did, but he has since told me that he was one of the first to sell Hi-Fi equipment at a discount in the UK. He did this from a shop in London so that's probably why I do not remember seeing much of him.

Eventually, after days of prickly anticipation after a phone call from Mum, she turned up on her noisy bike to get me. I was so glad to see her but by that time I did not really want to leave Cornwall, or Doe, or Kenny. We had a few more days at the beach with Mum and then we left. I was a bit cross with Mum for leaving me for so long, but I was also cross with her for coming to get me and taking me away.

I went willingly, however. I was still hers no matter how long she stayed away. My memory of my Mum that day on the beach before she left has grown in importance for me over the years. There is a song sung by Don Henley which has tugged at me every time I've heard it. It is an emotive song, so it probably would do that anyway, and it has a good strong melody. But I think I have figured out why I like the song so much. It reminds me of that golden day, of how I felt, and of my intentions towards my Mum. The song is called Boys of Summer. I can see my mum, sunglasses over her green eyes, skin glistening in the sunlight. I knew that my love for Mum would still be strong, even after all the men of all her summers.

# 12

# THE SUPERNATURAL YEAR

'Mary's house became a refuge for various hippies; the home was broken into on occasions. There appeared drawings on her walls and crosses placed upside down.'

Miss B S B, Social Worker, Derby Social Services. September 1978.

*

We travelled back to Derby via London on the motorbike and visited my name's sake, Dominic the Monk. This was the beginning of our supernatural year. We arrived mid-afternoon. As the bike spluttered out its dying breaths, Mum kicked the stand out and propped it up. As I took off my helmet I could smell the dank air with hints of decay in it, rising from the old London sewers. We were parked in the shadow of a row of huge, tombstone-white, terraced houses. There were steps up to every front door, with basements lurking below to the sides. There were four, if not five, storeys of massive windows, each with thick white stone sills. Mum ascended the nearest steps, helmet in hand, and pressed the round buzzer. Eventually out came a man with long, dark hair and a rock-star face. He wore a long, robe-like dressing gown.

'Dougie, this is Dominic the Monk. You were named after him. Dominic, this is my son.' Mum was looking at me and smiling.

'The Hound of Heaven.' The Monk looked at me with his dark eyes. 'Dominic was a hound, who went around heaven with a lantern looking for lost souls and guiding them back. The Hound of Heaven.'

I suddenly felt a great sense of purpose, that somehow I was destined to be like this heavenly dog. The man had a spiritual air about him and he spoke his words slowly with meaning.

'Are you a monk?'

'I used to be a monk but I'm not now. Well I am, sort of, but not like a monk who lives in a monastery. Life is a monastery.'

The Monk ushered us inside the door. As the door closed behind me I picked up the smell of baking potatoes. Mum and the Monk climbed the bare wooden stairs rising before us and I followed on behind them.

The old Victorian house had lots of bare wooden stairs inside, with flaking white paint at the sides, and many rooms. It smelt damp, with green or brown watermarks on the walls in places where pipes had leaked or rain had soaked through from outside. All the windows were tall, letting light stream in through the ones which had their dark curtains pulled back. The smell of the baking potatoes led us into the kitchen which had long strips of clear lino on the wooden floorboards, and pots and pans hanging from a pot-rack suspended from the middle of the high ceiling. The kitchen was warm, and homely with spider plants on the sills and shelves, their leafy babies dangling.

After baked potato, beans and cheese, I had the run of the house and garden, apart from the bedrooms. There was a lounge on one of the upper floors, with a huge empty fireplace and some sofas. It was full of strangers lounging and smoking.

The garden was thick with green bushes and small trees, making my entry feel like I was somehow crossing a threshold. Towards the back, near the border to the next garden, I found a rope swing attached to a tree. It creaked but held as I swung in the dappled light. I felt like I had been in this garden before. The pieces of fallen brick wall, black metal railings, the dappled light, and the old musty smell of rotting leaves, all seemed familiar somehow. It was like this feeling had crept up on me, had waited until I was all alone.

As I stopped the swing with my dragging feet, the back door of the house seemed suddenly unreachable. I sat, looking around, waiting to see someone observing me from the shadows. An eerie feeling enveloped me. What had been an unexplored jungle now felt like an ancient, familiar place and the veil between me and the unknown felt uncomfortably thin. Why did this place feel suddenly ancient, brooding, familiar? It was as if I had watched it slip from its former glory to become neglected and overgrown. I stood up, and retreated back to the steps as fast as I could without completely panicking.

'Mum, Mum, I've just been in the garden. I felt like I've been here before.'

The Monk nodded slowly. 'Yeah, that's deja vu little Dougie. It's like you've already seen it, already lived it before.' He smiled at me and then turned to Mum. 'Maybe your son's been here already Mary, in a past life?'

The one night spent as a guest in the Monk's house, with his many friends, was a long night for me. It was one of those nights when I was mostly free to do what I wanted. I hung around on the stairs and the landings between flights of stairs and struck up a friendship with a younger girl with blond pigtails. By the time it was starting to get light, I ended up in a room on a bare mattress with only my coat for a cover. The girl was in a cot next to me, finally asleep.

By the time we left Dominic the Monk's house, the sun was reflecting brightly off the cliff-like row of white houses. The street still smelt of sewers as Mum rode off and waved goodbye to my namesake. The smell only added to my feeling that I was leaving a familiar, yet uncomfortable, place.

*

We were greeted by not one, but two cats when we got home to Martin Street. The new cat, a tabby, did not belong to Mum but had 'decided to stay for a while'. Mum told me this, not the cat. I bent down and stroked its soft fur, wondering where its real home was, and if the owner was missing it. The first thing I noticed when I entered the house was that a wall had been knocked through from the hall into the lounge, making a window-shaped hole beginning at the height of my shoulder, draped with beads like the ones in the kitchen door. It felt like coming back to a different house. It had a different feel to it, maybe a different atmosphere.

There were still lots of people in the house, some familiar but some new faces as well. There was one lady, who liked to be naked nearly all of the time, whom I found interesting and unsettling all at the same time. She looked at me, holding out a white paper bag in front of her thin, pale body.

'Go on, try one. They're Indian Milk Sweets, all the way from India.'

I took one of the soft sweets from the bag and put it in my mouth. It tasted too sweet and oddly milky, not what I was expecting despite the lady's accurate description. I stayed as close to Mum as I possibly could.

On our return to Martin Street, Mum seemed

more restless than she ever had before. There were still the late nights in the house but Mum would go out more often and had started to take me with her rather than leaving me with others in the house. One night we set off together into town, which was a walk away, to look for 'dog ends'. When we got to the library, Mum picked something up from the floor – the stub of a used cigarette.

'Like this, only bigger. If you see any, pick them up and give them to me.'

We walked and crouched forward, searching the lamp-lit pavements. Eventually we ended up talking to a dark-haired man outside a restaurant, who gave Mum a cigarette. There was a white marble statue by the entrance of a woman holding a vase on her shoulders. The man looked like a waiter, with his black trousers and shoes, white shirt and apron. He leant on his broom smiling at me as Mum became more and more vocal and demonstrative with him. He kept smiling at me. I felt cold, tired and strangely lost as I watched them argue. I cupped my hands together on the dark windows and peered inside. There were rows of tables set with cutlery and candles, all empty. When we left the man at the restaurant, Mum grumbled and complained and told me that she 'thought that he would help us', but it didn't feel like he did. The whole incident felt more loaded somehow than it should have. I knew I didn't know everything there was to know about the dark-haired waiter with the white apron.

Another night, Mum woke me up and said, 'We've got to go and see Roger.' Roger was the vicar at St Wurburgs Church, which was in town before you got to the library. Mum had an unusual sense of urgency about her. We set off into the cold night, my eyes still half closed. When we reached the church, Mum knocked on the door of the vicarage. There was no answer, so she knocked again. It was spooky waiting in the dark in the graveyard. After some louder, more persistent knocks, the door opened and a small, white haired man in a dressing-gown peered out at Mum and I. He looked funny and lost in his pyjamas. I was used to seeing him in his black shirt with white dog collar.

'Hello Mary. It's the middle of the night. What can I do for you?'

'I think I need you to pray for me. I think I've got a demon.'

The small man disappeared into his house, then reappeared with a bunch of long keys. We followed as he shuffled over to the side door of the church. He fumbled with one of the long keys, which didn't work, so he tried another. Eventually the heavy wooden door creaked open and in we slipped. Lights were switched on and down the corridor we went to a room on the left at the bottom. We went inside the room which had a huge, worn rug almost filling the floor from wall to wall. Mum took a seat on one of the three large armchairs draped with dusty pillows and frilly armrest covers. I climbed into the one in the corner furthest away from the door and Roger the vicar followed in, closing the door behind him. As he sat in the armchair closest to the door, he looked small and far away. That night some peculiar things happened in that room. What I saw and heard next had a context and a build-up for Mum, but I was not aware of that at the time. Maybe I had seen the dots, but I had not joined them together.

At Martin Street there had been a picture of Jesus on the wall, which had been familiar to me either from my time with Grandma and Granddad, or perhaps Mum had put it up after they had died. When we returned from Cornwall, Mum said that she was going to throw the picture out. I complained about this.

'It's his eyes. They follow you around the room, haven't you noticed? Here, come and stand over this side of the room.'

Mum grasped my shoulders and I looked at Jesus' eyes on the wall. They were looking straight at me, even though I was at the very edge of the room. Mum walked me across the room, guiding me by my shoulders. 'See, don't they follow you?'

All the way through the middle of the room, over to the opposite side of the room, I kept my eyes fixed on his eyes. Sure enough they followed me all the way across the room. I shook free of Mum's hold and reversed track back across the room, watching the picture's eyes follow me to where I had started. And back again, looking at the eyes. I was so amazed that I grinned. 'How does it do that?'

'See? It's freaky isn't it? Wherever you go in the room, the eyes follow you around. Grandma used to tell me that God sees everything you do.'

'Does God see everything you do?'

Mum took the picture down and put it by the dustbin outside. I wondered if Jesus was okay being by the bins and if we had done something bad.

Then there was the cross. We had a crucifix on the wall, which had a statue of Jesus hanging on it. My memories of this crucifix are so hazy that I cannot truly tell what actually happened and what I have made up in my imagination. Mum was re-arranging it – that is a fact. Mum had a hammer and some nails – that is also a fact. I seem to recall that Mum was somehow struggling to get it to do what she wanted it to do. I could not say if Mum was trying to hang it upside down, or to get it to stay up the right way, but I remember, or seem to remember, the cross swinging on its own. I also seem to remember one of the nails jumping out of the wall onto the floor with Mum and I standing well back. This of course could all be my own imagination, filling in the gaps.

When I asked Mum many years later about that night with Roger she told me that weeks before she had been helping one of her friends to calm a woman down – a woman who had 'problems'. The woman had been thrashing around and flailing her arms and legs, and Mum and this man were trying to protect her by holding her down on the bed. When the woman had calmed down, Mum said that she was sitting next to her on the bed with her arm around her shoulders. Mum said that she felt something pass from the woman into her own body.

Then Mum told me about a picture she had drawn after her run-in with the woman. It was a drawing of a demon inside a house, a burning house with flames licking out of the windows. Contemplating the finished artwork had unsettled Mum so much that she had decided to burn it. She had set it on fire in a metal wastepaper bin. As the picture burned, black smoke had begun to pour out of the bin and billow into the room, and then into the rest of the house. Mum's take on it had been that the piece of paper had produced far more smoke than it should have done – black acrid smoke at that. Eventually Mum had retreated out of the house and called the fire brigade from a neighbour's house. I have no recollection of this event, so I presume it must have happened when I was summering in Cornwall.

Roger sat looking at Mum, listening as she spoke. I sat, head nodding, curled up into a tired ball on the soft armchair. Mum talked, and talked. Then they both closed their eyes and began to pray. Roger's tone of voice changed; he became more commanding, with added volume. Mum responded with a guttural moan. I began to cry. I wanted Mum to stop making those sounds and I wanted to go.

Roger turned to me.

'It's okay Dominic, this is normal, and it won't take long. This is going to make your mum feel a lot better. Jesus is going to set her free.'

I was now wide awake and held onto a dusty cushion as Mum's voice got louder. There was some conversation between Mum and Roger, but I cannot remember the content. Mum's voice no longer sounded just like Mum. Then the wailing, followed by the growling, started. It was similar to the girl with whooping cough in that it was a rhythmic, repetitive pattern, only these sounds were far more unnatural. Mum gripped both armrests with her hands, whilst her body flung forwards into a low, stooping motion. Her back was too straight, and her head was way too low, chin up and neck outstretched between her akimbo knees.

'Woa-oo-woa-oo-wao-oo wao. Grrrrrrr. Grrrrrrrrrr.'

'Woa-oo-woa-oo-wao-oo wao. Grrrrrrr. Grrrrrrrrrr.'

I sat in the corner terrified. Mum's body was contorting into unnatural positions which seemed too physically awkward for her to be doing. She was growling and wailing like an animal, like a wolf, or a lion. And the worst part was that all of this was happening to my mum, and I was worried about what exactly was happening to her.

Eventually Mum stopped wailing and sat up. Roger told me that I could give my mum a hug now.

Mum was smiling and thanking Roger as we left the musty room.

'Don't thank me. Thank Jesus because he has set you free. Hallelujah!'

'Hallelujah!' Mum said with her palms and face turned up.

'What's Hallelujah mean?'

Roger looked at me. "It means Praise the Lord! *Hall-ail* means 'Praise', and *jah* stands for 'God'. *Hall-ail-lu-jah*."

'*Hall-ail-lu-jah*!'

'Yes that's right. Keep on praising God! It will keep the Devil away. He hates it when people praise the Lord.'

*

On the way back through the darkness, I asked Mum "Why were you growling like that and bending over Mum?"

'I've had deliverance. I think I had a demon cast out of me.'

'What's deliverance Mum?'

'It's when you get set free from a demon.'

'What's a demon?'

'It's like a little devil, one of his foot soldiers.'

'Is it gone now then?'

'Yes, I think it's gone. It came out when Roger told it to go.'

'Did you feel it come out?'

'Yes, I felt it come out.'

'What did it feel like when it came out?'

'It was like I had retreated to the top of my head. It was like I was there but not there. Like I was looking down and watching myself. I saw these lines of colours coming out of my mouth – lines and bars of colours, all different colours. It was like I could see the sounds that I was making coming out of my mouth. But I feel much better now.'

When we got back to Martin Street, I was too scared to go to bed on my own, and Mum decided that we should sleep in the living room in two armchairs pushed together. As I dozed off, I snuggled up to my mum as close as I could. As I drifted off to sleep I dreamt that the Devil was looking at me from behind the high back of the armchair. As I woke up I could see him, in my mind's eye, crouching low behind the chair at my back, stooping and then disappearing with a fading growl. I was glad when the early morning light crept into the room and pushed back the darkness. Eventually I drifted off back to sleep, next to Mum.

*

1977 was the year when for me, the veil between the seen and the unseen became a little thinner. It was like living in a borderland, on the edge of, well, something else. Attending St Wurburgs Church only added to this feeling. Since the exorcism, Mum had started to go to church more often. We would go to the evening services in the old stone church, where people played guitars and flutes at the front. There were always candles burning brightly in the dimly-lit hall with stained glass windows and stone pillars. The grown-ups would go up to the altar at the front for prayer, and Roger and other people would put their hands on the people's heads, or their shoulders. Mum left me playing on the carpet while she went for prayer herself.

She stood patiently in a row of people which slowly moved forward as the rows in front passed on. When Roger put his hands on people, they were falling backwards as if they were suddenly asleep and being caught by people standing behind them, waiting for the catch. Mum was moving closer to the front, closer to those who fell and were dragged away and laid out on the floor. As I watched, I suddenly wanted to be with Mum, not on my own watching her fall backwards and being dragged away like a dead person. Whichever grown-up was with me at the time held me back and tried to reassure me.

'Don't worry, Mummy will be OK. She'll be slain in the Spirit. It's a bit like falling asleep.'

'What's 'slain'?'

'Erm, it's like resting in God's Holy Spirit.'

Mum reached the front and Roger and the others moved along the line, praying. I kept my eyes fixed on Mum. He got to Mum, put his hands on her head and, sure enough, back she went into the catcher's arms. I could see that she was smiling as she was dragged away and laid out on the carpet. I relaxed, relieved that someone had caught her.

I loved being in church. Apart from the soft carpet and the nice-smelling wooden seats there was an atmosphere, a presence, that I liked. The music was mellow and melodious. People were happy - not stoned-happy, this was different. People really were happy and peaceful. There was talk of God, or the Father, and Jesus his son. And the Holy Spirit, who laid people out on the carpet to rest. I was only six. I didn't really understand everything that was going on, but this was the time that I started to have my own thoughts about God, and the Devil, and angels and demons, and a whole other world that was seemingly hidden from sight. Yet I could sense it somehow, sometimes. Maybe on the edge of sleep, or beside a stone pillar amidst a chorus of singing, or when a grown-up was describing a vision they had seen.

Mum had got herself a pushbike and used to cycle it around with me in a plastic seat on the back. Some trips took us across town to an unfamiliar area. We would go to what Mum and others called 'house group', which was in fact in someone's house. There is one such occasion which sticks vividly in my mind.

The lady played the guitar and we sang on and on and on. I loved listening to the singing and watching the lady's fingernails pick the strings. Most of the people in the room were familiar people from church whose faces I recognised, but this wasn't church. It was someone's house, which smelt like someone's house, not like church. There was washing drying on an airer and baby's toys on the floor. When the singing finally stopped the man started to tell us about a vision he had seen.

'I went to heaven and I saw Jesus. It was shining everywhere and there was this flowing river. Then I saw him, standing right in front of me with his hands stretched out towards me. I could see his face. I could actually see his face. He had a beard and his face was shining.'

Whilst the man was talking I could almost see what he was describing.

'Jesus said, 'If you look into me, you will see the Father'. So I did. I looked into him and I saw the Father. It was like Jesus was a window to the Father. Then Jesus said 'I and the Father are one. If you've seen me, you've seen the Father'. It was like wow, I had seen the Father. They were the same. Jesus and the Father.'

I can still see this mind-movie playing out in my head to this day. Jesus, and through him, the Father, just like Jesus. I became aware of this idea that Jesus wanted to show us his Father. That he wanted to share his Father with us, with me. Mum and I talked about this on the way back home, savouring the atmosphere of the house group.

'Is God our Father?'
'Yes he is.'
'So is Jesus our brother?'
'Yes he is.'

*

Towards the end of our journey, Mum had a spiritual vision of her own. There were huge cranes in the centre of Derby which we could see from the hill we were walking down. By this point Mum had dismounted and was pushing me along still in the seat whilst she walked alongside. She looked at the cranes and stopped and stared. She pointed to the looming cranes.

'You see the cranes? They look like crosses, don't they? The one in the middle – can you see the diamond in the centre of it? It's like a mirror. It's a diamond-shaped mirror. It's like the cross of Jesus has a diamond-shaped mirror on it.'

When we got home, Mum got her art material and some paper out and began to draw. She drew a picture of Jesus on the cross, with a diamond-shaped tinfoil mirror where his face should have been. I helped her to cut some strips of dark material which she stuck around the mirror like hair. When it was finished she held it up in front of me. I knew it was meant to be Jesus but it didn't look, or feel like him.

'What do you see in the diamond?'

'It's a mirror.'

'Get closer. Look into it. What do you see now?'

'It's my face.'

'It's you. It's me. It's all of us. God showed me that it should have been all of us. When I saw the crane, I saw Jesus on it, like he was on a cross. But where his face should have been there was a diamond-shaped mirror instead. It should have been all of us.'

I got it. It made sense. I even believed it to be true, that we should have been on the cross instead of Jesus. He didn't deserve it, but we did. He was the only one who could pay the price. But there was something unsettling about Mum seeing diamond-shaped mirrors, and giant Jesus' on cranes.

I saw the cranes too. I felt the feeling, same as Mum did. But the dark sky behind the shining cranes stuck in my mind.

# 13

# INDIAN DREAMS

'It seems that her house was raided by the police on 9th September 1977, in a search for drugs. It is not clear whether drugs were found on this particular occasion but it seems certain that Mary both mixes freely with drug users and indeed takes drugs herself. Mary talked of her intention to travel to India and to send for Dominic once she had made preparation for him.'

Report dated 8th August 1979. B M, Social Worker.

*

Towards the end of 1977 Mum got together with a new boyfriend called Mike. It didn't last very long with Mike. He looked like Superman in a permanent state of 'Clark Kent'. He had a neat white sports car, with cramped seats at the back that I had to climb into. He made an effort with me, especially at Christmas. He filled the front room with toys – a wigwam tent, suede Native Indian outfit with tassels along the arms and legs, complete with moccasins, feathered head-dress, bow and arrows and quiver –

as well as loads more toys stuffed into the wigwam. He got Mum involved in his amateur-dramatics production by asking her to paint some of the scenery, which she loved to do. We took portions of the giant's castle wall home where Mum and I painted the leaves of the beanstalk onto it together.

Mike took Mum out on dates and left me with babysitters when he could. There was one evening when they wanted to go to the funfair together. Mistake number one was telling me where they intended to go, without me. Mistake number two was trying to leave me on my own with the strange naked lady with the Indian milk sweets, which I still didn't like. When Mum and Mike left, Naked Lady offered me a naked cuddle, and a milk sweet, and I screamed in her face. Mr Naked Man, who sort of came as a package with Naked Lady, was lurking somewhere around in the other room. Fortunately Mum heard me screaming as she was about to leave and came back for me. That night I was the prickliest gooseberry ever and Mike didn't thank me for it. The evening ended in hospital after I walked into a lamppost and cut my eyebrow open. They gave me three stitches to close the wound. Mum witnessed one stitch, then fainted – not the evening Mike had hoped for.

All my memories of Mike were of him and Mum together and me on the outside. It's like I suddenly had to interact with him all the time and Mum was somehow kept at a distance. The best thing I remember about Mike, apart from his Christmas tee-pee, was when he took us to a rock festival in his sports car.

On the way there were winding country lanes. It was good to see Mum having fun in the front as he drove the car fast from side-to-side through the bends. We stopped off at a pub on the way, with a huge standing stone nearby which Mike said was the stone from which King Arthur had pulled the magical sword Excalibur. I knew that it was the very same stone.

At the festival there was a triangle stage with men on it playing guitars. I went into the pen with Mum and Mike where the stage was but I didn't last long before I started to cry. I sat on Mike's shoulders with my hands over my ears because the noise hurt. Away from the stage was much better. I could still hear the music at a comfortable distance and there were lots of other interesting things going on. I slept in someone's tee-pee, a real full-sized tee-pee. There were people washing clothes in a stream, and half-naked women wandering around feeding babies on the breast. There were guitars playing and people singing beneath the tall thin trees. I played in the water and the mud with other strange but friendly children.

In the evening Mike drove us up the side of a hill in his sports car. I could see the campsite below with all the twinkling fires, and the stars came out one by one through the evening haze. Mike told me that the lights were fairy-fires and I believed him. I watched them both standing together, holding each other's hands. Mum was happy and I hated Mike a lot less than I did at first. Could this be it? Could Mike and Mum really be happy together? This was the night when I thought I saw Mike's straight-laced world collide happily with Mum's far-out magical and mystical world. It could just well work out. Just.

Mike disappeared after New Year of 1978, along with his white sports car and all of my Christmas presents. Mum told me that she couldn't keep them and that she didn't want his money anyway. She said that Mike was 'too nice' for her. Despite the rivalry between me and Mike for Mum's attention, I was cross with Mum for saying that he was 'too nice'. If Mum didn't want 'nice', what did she want? I found her statement unsettling because I thought that I was nice and began to wonder if I also was 'too nice' for her. After Mike, Mum turned her attention to more distant shores.

*

The idea of going to India grew in Mum's mind and became a dream and a goal of hers. Furniture started to disappear from the house – the sewing machine, the telly, the sofa. Early 1978 saw Mum and I alone again but at least together alone. I had not seen Dad since he visited me in Porter Road Children's home, and I was listening to different music now – two Jamaican girls singing 'love is all I bring, in a mi khaki suit an' ting' and the electronic tones of Mr Blue Sky.

Mum enlisted me into the fundraising effort for our new life in India together.

'Dougie, we won't be able to fit all your toys into our cases. We need to travel light. We're gonna have to sell them. We need as much money as we can get anyway.'

It was exciting at first, seeing all of my toys laid out on the grey blanket on the front yard, and preparing to be a shopkeeper. This was 'all for India', an exciting adventure just waiting for Mum and I to experience together.

'Put the labels on the floor by the things for sale. If someone offers you something near the price, take it. Just ask me if you're not sure.'

At first I was motivated to sell all of my toys for the higher purpose of an international adventure with my Mum. There they all were, neatly spaced and labelled – my Star Ship Enterprise which went round and around on a metal wire, my die-cast metal Thunderbird Spaceships, the huge box of Lego, both Action Men, complete with extensive wardrobe. Mum's trinkets were scattered around as well between the toys – bangles and necklaces, and Mum's Gurkha knife in its sheath I used to enjoy playing with. As I sat in the shade of the house waiting for people to come by and look at the sale, I began to get cold. Even before the first toy was walked away by a school friend, or some random kid who I'd never seen before, I was having second thoughts. I felt tricked and betrayed. I didn't want to have to go around to Darren or Gary's house and play with toys that used to be mine.

'Dougie, you've got a customer. Serve the lady. Do you want it in a bag?'

I watched as my toys were snapped up one-by-one, and taken away. My heart felt heavy but I tried to keep it to myself.

With 'India' on the horizon, the food menu began to change as well and Mum and I began to eat out together at Indian restaurants. I sat facing Mum across the table laid with white tablecloth and blue napkins. Her fuzz of dark hair was framed by deep red patterned wallpaper. To my right was a small flight of stairs leading up to a white hatch in the wall. Every now and then a bell rang as the hatch opened. Food was placed on a shelf and then transported by a waiter to a table but not ours yet. The smell of other people's curry was making my tummy rumble. At last the bell rang for our food which was hot and spicy and filling. I ate with Mum, as music with sitars and melodic female voices played loudly. At other times Mum and I would wait in the takeaway area, talking to the waiters or the barman. I began to love Indian restaurants and Indian food.

The most memorable meal was the one Mum and I ate around the back of the restaurant. We sat at a round table with an old man dressed in traditional Indian attire. There was no table cloth, or napkins, just forks, glasses, and a jug of water. I was cold and tired but I knew that food was on its way. The walls were bare and it did not smell as nice as the restaurant at the front end of the building where we usually had the privilege of dining. Although the old, wiry man was not familiar to me he spoke to 'Mary' as if he had known her for years. Eventually he disappeared and soon returned with mincemeat curry with peas and a plate piled with soft white chapattis.

'In India, we scoop the curry with our chapatti, like this.'

He ripped a triangle of chapatti from the plate and demonstrated.

'If you find the curry too hot, eat some plain chapatti to cool down. If you drink water while your mouth is still hot, it will burn even more.'

I was hungry and the meat and chapatti tasted delicious, if a little hotter than I was used to. It made my nose run, which Mum said was a sign that it was a good curry.

'Good curries always make you sniff.'

As we ate, the Indian man talked to Mum but looked at me, smiling kindly.

'He can be married in India when he is nine. He can marry a pretty bride and he will have lots of money. They allow marriage much younger in India than they do in this country.'

My mind was suddenly bursting with images and questions. 'Can children get married in India?'

'Oh yes, they can. This happens a lot in India. It is normal.'

'What would I have to do when I'm married?'

'You would put on fine clothes, Indian clothes,

and you would ride in a carriage with your beautiful bride. There would be flowers and music and lots of nice food.'

'Then what would I have to do?'

The man turned back to Mum. 'The boy would stay in India for a while. Then he would return.'

The idea excited me. Images of me and a young bride in a carriage filled my mind. There was food, flowers, and gold everywhere and everybody was Indian and rich. I was the star, along with a girl, who made it all possible. I would be married and rich. Married – this was the exciting and terrifying bit. I did not feel confident that I would be good at 'being married' because I did not know how. The images in my mind now showed me confused and helpless, not being able to remain confident or happy. Suddenly 'India' became shrouded in uncertainty and potential danger. That day's free bite of food had turned into a potentially destiny-changing encounter. I remained curious but unsure about the whole idea.

*

My memories of the summer months of 1978 are sketchy. I do not recall my seventh birthday. Before I had the luxury of my care notes, which provided me with a timeline, I could not have said for sure which parts of my childhood I did, or did not remember. One of the most unsettling things about having a concrete timeline is realising that there are periods where I remember almost nothing.

My memories of my imaginary Indian wedding are so vivid that I could almost believe it actually happened. There I was dressed in white, complete with white turban, sitting in an elaborately padded and decorated horse-drawn carriage. A girl dressed in yellow with long black hair sat beside me with a garland of white and yellow flowers around her neck. It was hot, with the sun beating down upon us. There were unfamiliar smells and people, lots of people, throwing petals at us. Yet this had all been a daydream in the back room of an Indian restaurant in Derby. For me this is a lesson about the unreliability of memory. But perhaps I did go? Maybe the sun and the horses with white plumes were real after all.

I can see from Mum's old passport, gifted to me by my eldest sister, that Mum was in fact issued a 10-year passport from Liverpool Passport Office on 19th July 1978. Mum did buy a passport that very year, no doubt in preparation for our trip to India. In my care notes, dated 19th September 1978, 'Miss White's' future address is noted as Swami, Arrand Sanjaya, Shree Ra Nkayegaom Park, Pune, 411 – 001, India. The actual address of Osho International, which is the same place as the Bagwan Shree-Rajneesh's ashram, is 17, 1st Lane, Koregaon Park, Pune, 411001, India. This is the location of the 'gate-less gate', which still stands to this day. Mum had dreams of joining the Ashram in 1978 and somehow finding herself beyond the gate.

There are visa stamps on Mum's passport but none for India. The only barrier between me and a 100% sure knowledge that neither I, nor Mum, ever travelled to India are three paperclips still attached to the visa pages of Mum's passport. The paperclips are empty, still pointlessly attached to the page. What they once held is a mystery. I am fairly sure that I never actually made it to India but I am uncertain about Mum. The reality of early to mid 1978 is that I remember snippets, which I think may have occurred around this time, although I can't be sure.

There were far more visits to other people's houses. Mum left me in one house, with a young blonde-haired man. It was daytime and I was left alone with a very strange magazine which had a picture of a lady talking on a red telephone. In 1978 telephones were attached to curly wires. The curly red wire of this telephone disappeared into the lady's nakedness. I knew that the rest of the telephone could not still be at the end of the wire. When Mum came to collect me, it felt as if we were escaping somehow and that she had rescued me. It felt good to be back in the bright summer sunlight.

There was another house I hated going into. It belonged to the Ice-cream Man. Mum left me there and we played games like dominoes and Kerplunk in the lounge which had an arch knocked through into the kitchen and then we went to bed. I have images of time spent with the Ice-cream Man but they are distant and foggy. I have tried at times to remember more but the fog remains. In another house, I lie in an unfamiliar bedroom propped up on one elbow, colouring in Mum's drawing of a scaly dragon. Mum pops in every now and again to see if I'm asleep. Eventually Mum's friend pops in and gets into bed with me and gets up and out when Mum next pops in again.

The best strange house was the one with the attic room. Up the stairs we went to the top of the house, following a tall, slim man with dark curly hair. The attic room had sloped walls and ceiling, with a skylight open to the dark night sky. There were two men, who looked very similar, and Mum, and me. They sat with legs crossed as the loud rock music played. At a guess I would say it was probably Jimi Hendrix and Pink Floyd. The ceiling and walls were covered in posters of rock musicians, festivals and bands. The grown-ups sat cross-legged in a triangle passing a glass jug full of water and smoke with a long pipe attached to it between them. Each one sucked the pipe, inhaled, and then blew out a puff of white smoke. Mum patted the floor next to her and I sat down.

'You have to suck the pipe until the water bubbles. It's OK because the water cools the smoke down. Do it slowly and as long as you can. Do you want a try?'

I took the pipe, which reminded me of a cross between a recorder and a bungee rope, and I sucked as slow as I could. I watched the water in the glass bubble as I pulled the smoke through.

When it hit the back of my lungs I coughed and spluttered, gasping for air. 'I thought.. you said it... would be cooler!' I spluttered.

'It is Dougie. There, you've had your first hubbly-bubbly. Did you like it?'

'No.'

The rest of the evening in the attic for me was music and posters, and sleep on an oversized cushion on the carpeted floor. This is not my worst ever memory.

Contact with Derby Social Services must have been thin during this period as there are no entries in my records. One afternoon I was at school eating banana sandwiches and then lying down for an afternoon nap. I was woken early by a teacher and we crept over the sleeping bodies together. I was then in a school office being told that I was not going to go home to Mummy today but that I would go to The Mount and that everything would be okay. I cried because I knew what all of this meant. It seemed like it had been such a long time since I had had to be in a children's home away from Mum. Someone gave me a stuffed Pink Panther teddy.

'You can take it with you if you like. You can keep it, it's yours.'

'Okay.'

On 19th September 1978 I was received into care from 6 Dashwood street, an address which I do not remember. Dashwood Street in Derby is still there but numbers 2 to 8 have been knocked down. The Mount on Albany Road was a 'Specialist

Treatment Centre', and that is where Pink Panther and I were placed. There was a beautiful, haunting song that used to play on the radio around this time, which Mum said was about alien invasion and red weed. But for me it was about Mum because she was again blowing away from me like an autumn leaf. Justin Hayward sang Forever Autumn for War Of The Worlds which reached number 5 in the UK singles charts in August 1978. When the sun shines through golden leaves on a cold autumn day it can be full of the promise of warmth. With Mum, it always felt like an English autumn. Indian summer forever remained a dream.

# 14

# THE MOUNT

- Date admitted to care: 19th September 1978
- Relevant Act (and Section): 1948 Section I
- Reception to: Community Home
- Status (legit. Adopt.): Illegitimate
- Address from which admitted: 6 Dashwood Street, Derby
- Reason for care: Mother travelling to India. Left Child at The Mount
- School Attended: Firs Estate Juniors
- Achievements and social relations at school: a bright little boy, who makes friends easily
- Miss White's future address: Swami Arand Sanjaya, Shree Ra Nkayegaom Park, Pune 411-001, India.
- General home conditions: house has been sold. The house has been claimed by the building society
- Name of nearest interested relative or family friend: Mr Ted Burrows
- Name and address of Doctor: Dr Tuckley, 53 Harrington Street, Derby
- Present health and habits: Health good. Eats well. Night time enurises
- Milestones:

Delivery: Forceps

Post partum feeding method: Bottle
Talking: Early
Walking: Early
Medical history: Chicken Pox
Care by grandparents until 3 years of age

B S B, Social Care Officer. 27th September 1978.

Memo to Miss Brown on 24th October 1978:

'I should be grateful if you could make full enquiries as to the whereabouts of Miss Mary White, mother of the above named child, and let me have your findings in writing.'

Additional note made on 24th October 1978:

'Spoke to Miss Brown. Mother's whereabouts are unknown. Supposedly gone to India. However, Miss Brown thought that The Mount might have an address for mother.'

Memorandum from Principle Admin Officer on 27th October 1978:

'In reference to your letter re: the whereabouts of Miss White; the lady left her home at 142 Martin Street without informing the Social Worker of her movements. Miss White chooses not to associate with the Social Worker at present. Her present whereabouts are not known either to the Social

Worker or The Mount where Dominic is placed.'

*

I sat on a bed with little James and Tony Royce. Pink Panther was at my side in the small bedroom which looked out onto the garden. I was upset because no-one knew where Mum was, or if she was going to come and collect me. I had been to The Mount a few times before, but didn't know Tony Royce, or James, very well. James had black curly hair and thick glasses. He had more fun in him than his looks would lead you to believe. Tony Royce, who was the manager of The Mount, told James to look after me and that he had to go and do some things but would return soon. I felt empty. James was funny and attentive enough to be a distraction, but I couldn't focus properly on any other thought but 'Where is she? Where's my mum? When is she coming back? Why has she not come back yet? Is she okay?'

When Tony Royce returned we talked about the film Jaws. We were in Tony's room which he slept in when he was working at night, and he had a poster on the wall of the Jaws Shark towering over a lady on water skis. Tony told us what happened in the film, with some of the gory bits edited out, and he and James performed a duet of the theme tune: 'Da-da, aa-da, da-da, dun-dun, dun-dun...'

Tony Royce was a big, burly game hunter of a man. In my memory he always wore khaki shorts and a jungle hat, although in reality I'm sure he wore other clothes sometimes too. He had a flashing smile and a deep kind voice. Tony sat on the bed between me and James and read a story, after which he and James said goodnight and left me alone with the floppy panther. I had arrived at The Mount and my next adventure was about to begin.

*

Apart from James, who was actually a day visitor at The Mount rather than a resident, all the other boys were older than me, a lot older. Suddenly I was the baby amongst a crowd of rough, adventurous teenage boys. Some of them were warm and welcoming, a few were aloof, but none were harsh or unkind. I got to do most things that they did. The first time I fired a pellet from an airgun in the basement it kicked back and hurt my hand. With a little help from Tony and others I eventually got to grips with it and was putting more pellets in the dartboard than the surrounding brick wall.

We had proper football matches in the back garden with metal goal posts and shin pads and gloves. I played in goal most of the time, which I didn't mind. Tony was a Nottingham Forest supporter and the only one at that in The Mount. Everybody else supported Derby County, including me. Tony was a red tree in a herd of black-and-white rams and the others made him feel the isolation as much as they possibly could. The more time I spent with Tony, the more I warmed to him and soon he became my hero. It wasn't long before my allegiance changed, partly out of admiration and wanting to be like him, but also a small bit of sympathy. I didn't like seeing Tony getting bullied about 'Cloughie's clowns' alone. Soon it was me, Tony and Peter Shilton against the world.

I got to go on nearly all the boyish adventures, which usually involved eating fish and chips. Trips to the seaside were frequent, with games of 'who could spot the sea first' on the way in the mini-bus. One trip to Skegness saw a whole minibus full of boys and men singing 'Lilly the Pink' at full volume. There was one place we went to where we would always sit down in the restaurant and eat, rather than buying a takeaway. I was reliably informed by Tony and other members of staff about the quality of the food on offer.

'This is the best, THE best, fish and chips in the world, anywhere.'

And so it was.

Matlock Bath was not far away where the illuminated fairy garden shone at night on the other side of the fast river. We would walk past the lit-up statues of fairies and gnomes drinking super-nose-fizzing coke from red cans. Then we would eat fish and chips with mushy peas beside the outdoor goldfish pond as the leather-clad bikers revved and buzzed around us. I would sometimes wonder if I would see Mum on her Suzuki 250cc, but I never did see her there.

Tony took us to see Notts Forrest and Derby County football matches, where we would all eat chips and pies whilst standing on the terraces. When we returned to The Mount it was crunchy peanut butter on toast all round, re-toasted to make it hot and crispy. I would hill walk with Tony and the boys through icy Dovedale, over the stepping stones on the fast flowing River Dove which was swollen with melt-water. It had snowed heavily and everything was white and icy, and then dripping in the warming sun. Then up we went over snow-clad Thorpe Cloud, the highest mountain in the Peak District. Some of the boys slid down the other side in bin bags, but I stuck close to Tony's hand.

The cinema featured heavily during my time at The Mount. Apart from one random memory of going to see The Water Babies at Saturday Morning Cinema, I had not been much. Tony Royce and other staff members and the boys, loved James Bond. We travelled all the way to London once to see a triple bill of our hero. I know it must have been London because I remember them all having an in-depth conversation about what 'triple-X' films were after we began to see the neon signs with the three X's lit up in red. Despite getting slightly fidgety due to the amount of time I had to sit still, I found the three Bond movies mesmerising. He rode a car out of the sea onto a beach, fought with a huge man with metal teeth on a cable car, floated in a Space Shuttle, and chased a midget with an evil grin around a sailing boat. Then he did Kung Fu, crashed a speedboat, and nearly got poison dripped into his mouth whilst he was asleep. For me, Roger Moore will always be the original James Bond. In more recent years I have taken to watching James Bond at the cinema with my father-in-law, who is just as good a companion as Tony Royce.

Then there was *Star Wars*. The first time I saw it I fell asleep. When the whole place erupted with laughter I woke up with a start next to Tony, and pulled myself upright. It was the bit when Chewbacca growled at a mouse-like robot on the Death Star, which squeaked and scampered away. From that moment on I was transfixed. When Obi-Wan-Kenobi was ruthlessly executed by the evil Darth Vader I experienced real emotional turmoil and disbelief, but I got through it surrounded by the boys and the rest of the viewers. When Princess Leia kissed Luke Skywalker before he swung her over the chasm, I felt a flood of warmth. We all punched the air together with a loud 'yes!' when Luke finally used the Force and destroyed the Death Star. The second viewing was even better, and there was probably a third as well. Sharing *Star Wars* with Tony and the boys was an immense event in my seven year-old life, packed with emotion and a new sense of belonging. I could see all of my own emotions and life events being played out on the big screen – hope, abandonment, death, loss, fatherlessness, love, despair. It was all 'a long time ago in a galaxy far, far away', and yet it was also right there in the auditorium as I sat next to my very own Obi-Wan- Kenobi, Tony Royce.

*Grease* did not work out quite so well though, for me at least. Right up to the last minute, it was still undecided as to whether I should be allowed to go. Then the football game was stopped and all of the other boys, apart from me, were called in to get changed and ready to go. I cried, and kicked the ball moodily on my own into an undefended goal. I had been watching Saturday morning telly clips of John Travolta, and Olivier Newton-John, for weeks. I had seen them singing 'Summer Loving', crooning into each other's faces, I had witnessed Sandy singing about her love, alone on a swing under the stars. Surely I should be allowed to see the film. Surely. But it was 'too old' for me. Only for me. When the boys returned, they told me that I hadn't missed much, out of kindness I think, but I squeezed every bit of plotline and action out of as many interrogations as I could. To this day, I have still never watched *Grease* all the way through, so I still don't know what all the fuss was about.

The strangest adventure I ever went on with Tony and the boys was to see Aladdin at the theatre, with two actors from an old comedy on TV called *It Aint 'Alf Hot Mum* – Windsor Davis and Don Estelle. Don sang 'Whispering Grass' whilst Windsor made funny noises into the microphone and wiggled his eyebrows. Then they invited children onto the stage to sing, 'When Santa got stuck up the chimney'.

'Go on, go with them. You'll be fine.'

'But I don't want to sing on stage. I want to stay

here with you.'

'Okay, but you won't get a prize.'

My legs propelled me along but my mind was still rebelling and wanted my bottom to stay firmly stuck to my seat next to Tony. Once up on the stage with the boys, I felt like everyone was looking at me and listening to every fumbled, mumbled word I managed to squeak out into the microphone.

'When Santa.... got stuck.... up....'

I couldn't even see what Santa had to do with Aladdin anyway.

We each opened our 'prize' in the minibus on the way home. It was disappointing. The goody bag contained shaving foam, a Bick razor, and a pork pie. Eventually, Tony managed to convince me to try the pork pie and I ate all of it apart from the disgusting, cold jelly which I in fact quite enjoy now.

My favourite adventure with Tony and the boys was ice skating. We would go to the ice rink in Nottingham, exchange our trainers for shabby blue ice skates and then swish the evening away. I soon got the hang of staying upright and it wasn't long before I was speeding around the bends with body low and arms swinging. The best bit was when they would switch off most of the lights and play the music louder. Only the fastest skaters were allowed to whizz around the ice, after which I would be among the first skaters back on to make the most of the space.

There were other adventures too, which I half remember: helter-skelters and coconut stalls at

Nottingham Goose Fair, animals and adventure play parks at Dreyton Mannor Park, walking in mist and rain in Wales, and meandering through Sherwood Forest. For me, living at The Mount was like living a boy's best dream. Even though I still missed Mum and wondered how she was doing in India, I treasured the new world I had stepped into with my Pink Panther – a world of adventure, and big boys, and lots, and lots, of swimming.

*

James lived over the other side of Utoxeter New Road, not far away from The Mount. I had met him a few times before my admission to The Mount. He walked me all the way home once, to Martin Street. This must mean that I attended The Mount at least a few times before Mum disappeared, although I do not remember it this way.

I went home with James once to his house from The Mount over Utoxeter New Road. On the way we told each other jokes about musical beans making you toot, and the TV sports presenters Dickie Davis and Frank Bough. James' glasses were broken, taped together at the nose. He was the same age as me but he was smaller and slighter. When we got to his house no-one was in, so we slipped into his backyard and pulled up some rhubarb. We washed it in the flush of the outside toilet at the bottom of the garden, which James said no-one used as a toilet anyway now.

Although he did not live at The Mount, James was a frequent companion, and I missed him when he was not around. I got the feeling somehow that he had a harder life than me, but didn't understand exactly where that feeling came from. I didn't know much about his home life but I worried about him when he didn't show up for long periods. James would often come swimming with us all, when he was around.

Travelling to the baths and swimming in the pool were immensely enjoyable activities. It was on the night journeys back from swimming that I used to think about Mum the most. I had such strong memories of Queen Street baths, of seeing Mum at her happiest, smiling, with no weight of care or worry on her features. Even when I was swimming underwater, trying desperately to follow the slant of the bottom down into the deep end, I would wish that Mum could see me now, swimming underwater. I told everyone that my Mum had taught me how to swim, and how sneakily she had done it.

Sometimes we would go to Ripley baths, which was always warm, or other times we would go to Nottingham, which had a deeper deep end. Tony would push me down as far as he could so that I could touch the deepest part of the bottom, which made my ears pop. I loved the water and playing and splashing with the other boys. They were all bigger than me, apart from James, and we would both get thrown in the air and tossed around. I would swim underwater and try to get through

Tony's legs, or to tickle his feet. He would curl into a mushroom and me and James would bob him up and down. I remember the feel of his smooth, freckled back and his strong arms. Again the pool proved to be a well of positive physical contact, skin-on-skin. In a way it was still about nurture but of a different kind. Letting older boys, and men, into my personal space, and receiving affirming or even knockabout physical touch, felt good. Perhaps this was part of the 'Special Treatment'. Perhaps the therapy of positive masculine nurture and affection, including the physical, occurs at times unrecognised or unnoticed.

Journeys back from swimming were magical and sad at the same time. Everything was bleary and the lights on the motorway twinkled like stars through the chlorine-induced haze. The minibus filled with vinegar fumes and the smell of chips as we all scoffed on the way back. It was a time of reflection for me. Exhaustion can sometimes make a child more susceptible to negative emotions.

After dropping James off home, the minibus would climb up the slope of the driveway at the side of the house and Tony would shout 'Make sure all the windows are closed.' I would go to bed with the words of pop songs played on the minibus radio still echoing in my mind. 1978 was full of emotive songs, which all reminded me of Mum, especially because I didn't know where she was. There was one particular song by Renaissance called 'Northern Lights' which resonated louder than the rest. It reached number 10 in the UK charts in the summer of 1978 and was played on the radio for some time after. The video on Top Of the Pops had starry lights in it, just like the ones I saw on the motorways on the way back from swimming. But they never guided me back.

*

Tony Royce and James were by no means my only friends at The Mount. Bonds of varying degrees were made with most of the other boys, probably about eight or ten of them. I had different relationships with each. Some would ruffle my hair and slap me on the shoulder. Some would play games with me like Monopoly and give me a fighting chance of winning. They all tried to look after me as if they were my older brothers. There was only one time that I remember anyone being annoyed at me and that was during a football match when I didn't pass the ball when I should have. There was one particular boy who especially took me under his wing though, an older boy called Steve.

He would take me to visit his family sometimes and we would sing songs together as we walked along the streets. 'Gordon is a Moron' was a particular favourite of his. He told me that a girl that he really liked had dumped him for a man called 'Gordon' and that was why he loved singing the song. I think that this was the first time I had ever experienced romantic pain, albeit second-hand.

Steve wore glasses and had a flop of blond hair over his eyes. He also helped me to break my wrist at a disco-dancing party.

The boys spent ages preparing for the party. The basement room was dimly lit; the records were chosen and piled up. The snooker table had been moved out to make space for disco-dancing. Steve and I had practised our dance moves. Steve had a new girlfriend and all the boys were allowed to invite girls to the disco if they wanted. Steve's girlfriend had a little sister, who had also been invited. The routine was short and simple, and acrobatic; we had been practising it all afternoon. They would arrive, descend the stairs, sit, and watch in amazement. We would jive and Steve would pull me through his legs and flip me high into the air and let me freefall back into his arms. By doing this, he would impress his girlfriend and I would look amazing in front of his girlfriend's little sister. It was the perfect plan.

I wore a brown, full-collared shirt, and green flares. My shoes had been shined, and my mop of glossy hair brushed through. I waited in the gloom as the boys spun the records. 'Once, Twice, Three Times a Lady,' and 'If you want my body,' followed by 'If you leave me now, you'll take away the biggest part of me, oo-oo-ooo, no baby please don't go.' And then they arrived. Our pair was among the first to get there, slowly descending the basement stairs with dresses swishing. They smiled and sat. Steve grabbed me and we took to the floor.

'Good bye grey sky, hello blue. There's nothing to

hold me when I hold you. Seems so right, can't be wrong. Rockin' and rolling all week long.'

I rolled and swayed to the theme tune of Happy Days and then lay on the carpet. Steve stepped over me and grabbed my hands. He pulled me through and flung me high. Up I went, higher than I went during our practices, and down, down. Steve's hands touched me but fumbled. Down I went. Instinctively I put my hand out in front of me to break the fall and something gave way. Suddenly I was on the floor in immense pain, cradling my wrist in my other hand, crying, desperately embarrassed by my first, and worst, epic fail.

The small girl looked really sorry for me as I was taken off the dance floor injured. Later on, as I lay in my bed in pain, Steve came up and told me that the girls had left, but his girlfriend's little sister was asking if I was okay.

At first no-one realised I had broken my wrist. I lay in agony, drifting in and out of an uneasy sleep. When the sound of the thumping music downstairs finally stopped, the boys began to drift upstairs to bed. In they popped, one by one.

'How's your wrist?'

'It hurts.' Hot tears welled in my eyes.

'You did a good dance though.'

'Yeah.'

Eventually, Tony Royce came and sat on my bed and asked me to wriggle my fingers. I couldn't. So off to hospital I went.

After waiting on a bed on wheels in a hall for a

while, a doctor stuck a needle in my good wrist.

'Count up to ten and you will be asleep before you finish.'

'OK. One, two..... weeeeeeee!'

The world tumbled away around me as consciousness disappeared. It actually felt like being on a roller coaster and for about two seconds I was as happy as I had ever been, whimsical in fact. When I woke up, my arm was in a hard plaster-cast from half way down my upper arm all the way to my hand, my fingers and thumb protruding through the holes. Tony said that the doctors had needed to re-break the bone so that it would heal straight.

I returned to The Mount as a hero. Steve and Dom's dance was the talk of the place and the fact that I had endured three hours of pain in bed with a broken wrist went down in history.

The cast was heavy and got in the way at bath times. It eventually began to smell sweaty and my arm itched underneath it. Sports were off, including shooting in the basement. Instead I picked up all the squashed metal pellets for the boys with my good hand and twiddled them in between my fingers. All the boys and staff at The Mount signed my cast and some drew small doodles on it. Before too long it was full with repeat signings and pictures of Popeye and Micky Mouse.

When I returned to Firs Estate School, it was not to the infants. It was my first year of junior school, what would now be year three, and I had missed the start. I had missed a fair bit of school due to being away at various places, and at times a different school. Although Firs Estate Junior was reached through an adjoining gate from Firs Estate Infants, it felt like a strange, scary place, and I still had my plaster-cast on. My friends all wanted to sign it, but an older boy who I didn't know noticed all the names already on the cast.

'Who are all these people then?'

'My brothers.'

'Flippin eck, how many brothers have you got?'

The boy was laughing at me and sniggering to all his friends.

'I've got lots of brothers. And uncles.'

'You're a liar. You got all those signatures because you're in care. You live in a children's home you do.'

I had never tried to hide being in a children's home from anyone before and it had never been an issue. But suddenly I wanted to deny it, to defend the lie I had told. For the first time I remember, I didn't know what to say.

'Care boy, care boy. He's in a children's home!'

I wanted to punch him. Tears welled and I wished the ground would open up and swallow me back to The Mount. I really, really wanted to punch him. I got sent home early that day, either because I swore at him, or because I was upset. When I told the boys what had happened, they told me they would come to the school and sort the kid out if he teased me again like that.

Apart from breaking my wrist, my time at The

Mount was one of the best periods of my childhood, packed with good memories which have lasted through the years. Tony Royce used to tell me stories of a holiday that he took the boys on and that he wanted to take me on too. It was to a Scottish island called Mull. Tony showed me photographs of grey cliffs and stony beaches, and him and the boys in wetsuits with snorkels and flippers in hand. He told me about the mists, and the sea, and the wildlife. He wanted to take me to Mull and show me what he thought was the best place on earth. If only he had been allowed the chance to take me there, I would have travelled by minibus, and ferry, to that distant misty Scottish isle of Mull, with the amazing Tony Royce.

# 15

# TWENTY RED LIGHT DAYS

'Mary openly talked of her involvement in the drugs scene and offered to roll me a 'reefer'. Needless to say, that is not my weakness.'

B M, new Social Worker. 11th April 1979.

'Mary has altered in personality; she is on the one hand an intelligent, artistic person, another side is irresponsibility. The girl is as changeable as the weather; one cannot anticipate how she will react.'

Miss B S B, outgoing Social Worker.

*

The beginning of the end of my time at The Mount was when Mum abducted me from school on 16th January 1979. School was over and children were milling away from the teachers. It had begun to snow earlier and now big fat flakes were drifting slowly down into everybody's fresh footprints in the cold, white playground.

'Dougie. Dougie.'

I spun around, trying to see where the voice was coming from.

'Dougie! I'm over here.'

I spotted Mum outside the school gate, beckoning me with her hand.

'Come here Dougie, I'm taking you home. Well, come on then.'

I looked at her and froze. Then I looked back at the teacher who was talking to another grown-up. Then I looked back at Mum.

'Come on.'

I started walking towards Mum but kept looking back at the teacher for some guidance, hoping he would spot me. When I was near the open gate, I caught his eye as I turned around but it was too late. My stomach flipped as I broke into a jog through the gate. Even though I felt like I was doing something wrong, I ducked into the waiting car, engine running. I hadn't seen Mum for a while and although I was relieved and elated to see her, I was not sure I was quite ready for this. Her hair had grown even longer and fuzzier.

Inside the big brown car it was warm and fragrant, and the seats were big and comfy. Mum held my hand and beamed a smile at me as the two men in the front seats where the reggae music was coming from turned around and looked at me. The driver was a big West-Indian man with a hat on and a huge flashy smile. The passenger was smaller and had a tangle of dreadlocks stuffed into a stripy hat.

'Dis a ya bwoy den Mary? Im look like you.'

'Dougie, this is Duke and Rudii.'

Duke, the driver, laughed. 'Ha! You come an tek

de child from school Mary. A wah you'a like woman?'

I didn't say a lot but knew I was smiling way too much. Away we went, through the now heavily swirling snow. By the time we arrived at the unfamiliar house on Sale Street, there was a thick covering of snow on both pavements and street. I wondered why we were not going home to Martin Street. This house was dark and cold. Rudii started to dig a hole in the ground in the small space between the low wall and the house.

'We need some electricity around here. I'm gonna borrow a bit from de neighbours,' he said in a whisper with his finger over his lips. He dug, and dug, and eventually sat down on the ground and started prodding and poking around with his tools in the hole. Suddenly the lights in the house came on and Rudii punched the air and whispered, 'Yes I! Power to de people dem!'

Mum said she'd cook beans-on-toast and that I could go and play in the snow for a little while if I wanted to. I wrapped up in my snorkel Parker coat and set off into the blizzard. As I walked along the unfamiliar street the snow blew thick and fast, first this way, then swirling that way. It was mesmerising and calming. The motion sucked out all of my fear and soothed my anxieties. It was snowing and snowing hard, and everything was becoming white and cold. I knew that they would be wondering where I was at The Mount by now, but it didn't bother me greatly. I was alone in the snow and for a while it was magical.

I somehow found my way back to the house through the unfamiliar streets, after a slight panic when I realised I didn't know the number and was not quite sure which house it was. I eventually figured that it would be the one with the badly covered-up hole at the front.

'We've managed to borrow a bit of electricity from next door thanks to Rudii. I'll just get your beans-on-toast for you my love.'

Mum disappeared into the kitchen whilst I looked around the room. It was bare with no carpet on the floor, with an open fireplace that smelled of cold stone, rather than burning. Mum returned with a pile of beans-on-toast for me and I ate. It was not long after I had licked the plate clean that there was a loud knock on the door. Three police officers came into the house, two men and a woman. One male officer smiled at me whilst the other one told Mum off. She was looking sheepish. They all smelled of the cold night air and steam was starting to rise from their wet coats.

When they left, I wanted them to take me with them. But they didn't. As soon as I saw the police officers I thought my brief home visit would come to a sharp end and in fact, that is how I remembered their visit at first. In my mind I did go with the police. They had come to find me. They had rescued me from the coldness of unfamiliarity and uncertainty. But in reality that did not happen and they did not take me back to the Mount. They had come to investigate Rudii's un-orthodox brand of 'hole in the ground' electrician-ship.

What I now remember about my three days of 'abduction' is hazy and disjointed. We did not stay in the first house. I did not spend much time with Mum at all. Most of those three days were spent in a room with at least three other children. We were all talking about Duke, me like I hardly knew him and they like they knew him very, very well, possibly as a father. They would tell me to be quiet every time we heard people on the other side of the bedroom door. They spoke of Duke as if he were a feared disciplinarian who would be none too pleased if any of us made a sound when we heard the voices.

I remember two brothers and a girl. The boys were there almost all of the time but the older girl came and went. They all had afro hair and smelt of cocoa-butter and were pleasant enough. The older boy played his music to me on his record player. Gary Glitter 'D'ya wanna be in my gang, my gang, my gang?' He did a good impression of the singer whilst he jumped up and down on the bed and played air-guitar. The younger boy kept climbing onto the wardrobe and leaping off onto the bed shouting 'Geronimo!' I think I did the same a couple of times. There was also a lady who came and went, but didn't seem very warm towards me.

I do not know exactly how long I stayed in the room. I slept there at least once and began to want to get out of the stuffy, confining space. I know from my records that Mum took me back to The Mount three days after she took me from school.

Apparently I was dropped back off at The Mount on 19th January 1979 although I don't remember this event. Maybe I was tired or even asleep. Maybe Duke drove me, Mum and Rudii up to the drive and let me out before pulling a wheel spin and disappearing in a cloud of dust. I don't remember seeing any more of Rudii or Duke on that occasion, but as it turned out that was not the last time I would see the enigmatic Duke.

*

Life at The Mount continued as normal after the abduction but now that Mum's whereabouts were known there was a new uncertainty about my future. There are several addresses recorded for Mum in early 1978, all of which were close to the old Baseball Ground, which used to be Derby County's home football ground. It was also one of Derby's best known red light districts, which I did not know anything about at the time, explicitly at least. Eventually Mum discharged me from care at The Mount on 7th April 1979, thirteen days before my eighth birthday. I have no memory of leaving The Mount. No goodbyes, no packing and taking bags, just a growing sinking feeling that it would not last. The address I was discharged to was 56 Shaftesbury Crescent, which I now presume was Duke's flat, a stone's throw away from the Baseball Ground turnstiles. I had a new Social Worker called Barry Muir, who visited the flat on 11th April 1979, where he didn't share a 'reefer' with Mum.

I have no memory of arriving at no.56 but I have lots of memories of playing around there. The streets were at first unfamiliar, causing me to get lost more than once. The children were extra-friendly considering I was a stranger and most of them were Asian. We played football in the road a lot, especially on match days. There was a big buzz as droves of fans in football scarves poured down the streets and then through the blue turnstiles. There was a corner shop nearby which Mum sent me on shopping errands to and from which I tried to steal penny shrimps. I wasn't very good at it and eventually got caught running away with a pocket full. The shopkeeper shouted at me and gave me a ban, which I eventually sheepishly ignored.

When Barry turned up I was playing with some other children at the front of the house.

"Hello Dominic. Is your Mum in?"

"I think she's upstairs."

The bottom door was open, which gave entry to the long, straight stairs which took you up to the upstairs flat door. Barry disappeared inside and I carried on playing. Eventually an upstairs window opened and Mum's head popped out.

"Dougie! Come upstairs a minute. Barry wants to speak to you."

The flat did not look, feel or smell like it belonged to Mum. The living room had a glass table in the middle and scrappy sofas. There were huge silks hanging on the walls with elephants and tigers on them, surrounded by patches of wall with flaking paint, revealing bare plaster underneath. There was a stereo in the corner, which was always playing reggae music way too loudly. The whole place smelt like a big, Jamaican man – aftershave and cocoa butter; not unpleasant, just unfamiliar at first. Even the scent of cannabis was heavier and more pungent than it had ever been at Martin Street.

The lounge disappeared down a few steps into the kitchen at the back, passing the bathroom on the left. I never got to see much of Mum and Duke's bedroom, but I had my own little box room at the front. On match days I could hear the roars and chants from my bedroom window. My game was to try and figure out what the words of the chants were. This was hard and I knew that if Dad were here he would know exactly what they were saying.

Mum was thinner than I had ever seen her and her clothes didn't look like her own. The kaftans and leathers were gone, replaced by flimsy leopard-print tops and tight, shiny trousers. Mum had always liked wearing clogs and open-toed sandals, but now she mostly wore black high-heels. Her hair was shorter and tighter and her lipstick redder. She was the same, but different. As I entered the living room Mum rolled a cigarette on a record sleeve. Barry sat on the opposite sofa with his hands on his lap.

'How are you Dominic? My name's Barry. Do you remember me? I've just come to see how you and your mum are doing. They your friends out there?'

'Er, yes.' I looked at Mum who was licking along

the white Rizla paper and smiling happily.

'How are you getting along with your mum at the moment Dominic?'

'Fine. Am I going back to The Mount?'

'I want you to visit there sometimes, if that's all right with your mum.'

'Am I going back to The Mount, Mum?'

Barry answered for her. 'Well, we don't know yet. You really liked it there Dominic, didn't you? Maybe you could go during the day sometimes, you know, like James does.'

'What does he need to go there for now?' Mum asked. 'He's fine here with me. Money is tight, but we're coping, aren't we Dougie?'

Mum's smile was thinner.

'Yes Mum.'

I sat down on the carpet next to the glass table between Barry and Mum. Barry relaxed back into the sofa. He had long, thin legs and his knees were sticking up in the air.

'Well, it would be good if he could keep going every once in a while Mary. So Dominic, who else lives here with you and your mum?'

'Duke.'

'How do you and Duke get on then?'

'Okay.'

Mum's winning smile returned. 'I think it's good for him to have a man around to talk to. Duke is good with him. He's not around that much anyway. He works a lot.'

'What does he do Mary?'

'You know, painting and decorating, fixing stuff.'

'And are you working at the moment Mary?'

Mum laughed loudly and then looked at Barry. 'No, no. I'm just concentrating on me and Dougie. Who's gonna look after him if I'm out working all the day anyway.'

'Quite', said Barry.

Mum did go out a lot at night, and seemed to sleep a lot during the day. Getting ready for a night out had become a bit of a ritual for Mum. I had learned to recognise the different stages of the routine: a bath, with loud music, then wandering around the flat with a green towel on her head and a drink in her hand. The smells and the steam from the bathroom would fill the flat, making it warm and fragrant. She would then wander around looking for an afro comb, or nail polish, whilst telling me to stop getting under her feet. Then she would disappear into her room for a long time and I would watch the telly or go out to play.

Sometimes Duke would be around, sometimes he wouldn't.

I had a really interesting conversation with him once about saunas.

'Mary, am jus a gwan down to de sauna.'

He had a rolled up towel in his hand and looked ready for a swim.

'Is a sauna swimming?'

'It's probably a bit like swimming, yes, but not exactly de same.'

'Can I come then?'

Duke laughed out loud and slapped his thigh. 'You hear dis Mary? Ya bwoy wan fi gu down ti de sauna wi mi. Blouse-an-skirt! A wah ya bwoy a like een Mary?'

Mum shouted through the closed bedroom door. 'He's not going to the sauna.'

'Why can't I come then?'

'It's hot, an then cold. You get a steamy box den you jump in a de freezing pool. Everybody naked except for a towel.'

'Why do you jump into cold water?'

'It cleans all the badness out a de skin. You have fi sweat it out den wash it aff.'

'Sweat what out?'

'All de duttiness in a ya pores.'

'What's your pores?'

'Its tiny holes in a ya skin. When it's hot they open up and sweat out de dirt.'

'Do you wear swimming trunks?'

'Some do, some don't. All de ladies wear bikinis an' ting.'

'Why don't the men wear any trunks then?'

'Ho, bwoy. Curiosity killed de cat ya know.'

Duke laughed, and left, without me. I was disappointed that Mum would not let me go with Duke to the Sauna. We didn't even go swimming any more.

I did get on with Duke all right. He mostly ignored me and occasionally spoke to Mum about me, rather than to me. I didn't like the way he talked to Mum though sometimes. They would go into their bedroom and shout. Sometimes I would hear things smashing or banging. Once the door flew open and Mum staggered out around the table, spitting nails at Duke. Her clothes were dishevelled and her tears had streaked her mascara down her cheeks. Her lip was bleeding. My fingers did no walking in her hair. She was too busy with Duke and they hadn't finished quite yet. He followed her out of the bedroom still shouting at her. This time I was the one who cried because I understood some of what was happening. I jumped up off the sofa, trying to stay out of both of their way. It was worse when they went back into the bedroom and carried on shouting. It was worse not being able to see what they were doing to each other. I liked Duke less for this, for breaking my Mum down like I had never seen in quite the same way. Mum seemed more fragile somehow with Duke. She wasn't the one in control. He was such a big, powerful man with a presence about him.

Mum would often go out at night after her long routine, dressed up in black high heels and flimsy clothes. I would sit up and watch telly until I fell asleep on the sofa. This was the time that I developed a taste for late night horror films like Dracula, or Hammer House of Horror films about demons, or severed hands, or stranglers. I loved watching them, even the black-and-white ones. None of them were as chilling as Tales of the Unexpected anyway, or even as scary as Sapphire and Steel.

One night, Mum came back early, slamming the flat door loudly behind her and dumping two bags of shopping on the living room floor. She breathed heavily as she collapsed back into the sofa, staring into space.

'Her teeth fell out. I kicked the poor bitch's teeth out Dougie.'

"Are you okay Mum? What happened? Is she bleeding?"

'Yes, she is bleeding. She just made me so, so angry though.'

'What did she do Mum?'

'She thinks she can take my man. Well she's gonna have trouble doing that from hospital.'

'Did you do a karate kick on her Mum?'

'No... No. She was bending down shopping. I wasn't even looking for her. I just walked up to her and kicked her in the face. She probably didn't deserve it quite that bad. I think I might get into trouble for this.'

Mum looked at me, and then hugged me, crying. 'I think the police might come. I kicked her really hard Dougie.'

The police did come and ask Mum about the incident at some point and I was there because I remember seeing the policeman sitting in the living room. I do not know what was said or asked but Mum did not suddenly disappear to prison, like I feared she might.

I didn't tell Barry any of this stuff. Most of it was yet to happen, but even at the point of his visit I must have been feeling uneasy because I remember deciding to keep my mouth shut. In a sense, I didn't mind him knowing what was happening or how I was feeling, but I just knew that if I said too much it would mean more and more questions. I knew what I wanted to happen. I wanted Barry to have a nice chat with Mum and I, and then to leave happy. I knew that if he didn't leave happy, things would get complicated and I might have to leave Mum again. I had loved being at the Mount, but I was back with Mum now, which was even better.

'So, I will come back in about a week's time and check to see how you are both doing. Well, is that okay, Dominic?'

'Yeah.'

Mum put her roll-up in the big glass ashtray and pulled herself up. 'These sofas are old and some of the springs are broken. Could you get us any help with a furniture grant, Mr Muir?'

Barry looked around and nodded. 'I can't promise, but I will see what I can do for you. Goodbye Mary.'

He reached out and shook Mum's hand.

'Goodbye Dominic. Nice seeing you again.'

I watched him get into his car down the street from my bedroom window and then drive away. Part of me wanted to be in the car with him.

*

Food was important to me at 56 Shaftesbury Crescent. I ate lots of baked beans, spaghetti and toast – spaghetti on Marmite on toast, beans on buttery toast, fried egg on beans on toast. I had my eighth birthday whilst living there, but do not remember any celebration or cake or any other food apart from things on toast. After being caught stealing penny shrimps at the corner shop I tried my luck at the local Co-Op. I just picked up the bar of fruit-and-nut chocolate, pulled my coat up from the bottom, and stuffed it up inside my jumper. Then I just walked out. I wore a cloak of invisibility, powered by not looking directly at anyone. I was on my own, and I can't remember where I had got the idea to do this from. Once I was outside behind the wall at the front of the shop, I pulled the huge bar of chocolate out. I was looking at it, wondering if I should eat it all in one go, or save some for later, when I heard a voice behind me.

'I've just seen you take that bar of chocolate from the store without paying for it. Where's your mum?'

I spun around to see the tall, thick-set man in a blue uniform bending down in front of me with his hand outstretched, palm faced upwards. I quickly filled his hand with the fruit-and-nut bar and then belted away at a sprint. All I wanted to do was get out of his sight. He knew what I had done and I could feel his knowing eyes on me.

There was money around because I saw it. There were piles of paper notes on the glass table sometimes and Duke would sit and count it. I would often go on a shopping errand and come back with more notes than I went with, plus coins. I became adept at pricing up items and counting the change, as bringing back less money than I should from the shop meant me having to go back and ask the shopkeeper to make up the short-change.

I was once as an adult brave enough to ask Mum if she had sex-worked whilst living with Duke. It was an awkward and risky question but I wanted to know. Having worked in a professional capacity with street-based sex-working women, and the men in their lives, I had become familiar with some of the signs. Plus Mum had always been upfront with me that it was a red light district on the streets around the Baseball Ground.

'Did he ever make you sex-work, Mum?'

I was surprised how comfortable Mum had been with this question, even though she became just slightly cagey about it.

'No, no, he tried to get me working, but I refused. He had other girls that would work for him though.'

'What, other girlfriends Mum?'

'Nah, not girlfriends, just floozies that hung around him.'

'Was he ever violent to you, Mum?'

'Yes, a few times. But I gave as good as I got you know. He did have a temper though. But so did I.'

Of all the periods of time I spent with Mum in my childhood, she felt the least available to me whilst at no. 56. She was always behind a door, or getting ready, or with Duke. Both food and maternal attention were lean. There was never any competition between me and Duke for Mum's attention because I just didn't stand any chance. Mum was absolutely besotted with him and I was a house gooseberry.

Once I came home for tea. No-one was in the lounge and the music was blaring loudly. The kitchen was empty. No-one was in either bedroom. I felt a panic rise in my throat. Not just because no-one was around, but because the music was still on.

I knocked loudly on the closed bathroom door, it being the only room I hadn't yet tried. I heard no answer over the loud music so turned the handle and almost fell in down the two wooden steps on the other side. What I saw next shocked me. Through the steam I saw the back of a large black man, who was Duke, and a very pale-skinned Mum facing me in her full naked white glory. Both were standing facing each other in the bath, and it looked like Mum was washing Duke. Duke laughed. I apologised while still staring at the pair.

'Sorry, I didn't think...'

'Get out! Get ... out!'

Mum screamed at me as she tried desperately to cover herself. As I turned and left the bathroom, Duke said, 'Mary, no bother shout at de bwoy. Is all right ya know...' as I slammed the door shut.

I cried and cried. I felt so excluded, rejected and unwanted. Mum had been so angry with me for seeing her. She could bathe with Duke, even wash him, but I was kept at such a distance. I couldn't understand why she had panicked so much at the sight of me. I couldn't bear the thought that she could wash Duke in the bath but rarely ever hold me. Nakedness wasn't the issue for me; it was closeness and access.

When Mum came out in a towel and sat beside me on the sofa she made an effort to make things right again.

'Why are you so upset, Dougie?'

'You screamed at me to get out and I just wanted to know where you were because the music was on and no-one was in the flat.'

'You shocked me. You should knock before you go into the bathroom.'

'I did. No-one answered. How come you can wash Duke in the bath and not even want me to see you naked?'

'I'm sorry. I was just shocked. I don't mind you seeing me naked, I was just shocked.'

'Well you don't want me to see you naked because you yelled at me.'

'I really don't mind. Look, I need to finish my bath. You can come in and wash your face and brush your teeth.'

This was not the best idea Mum had ever had. If I could go back in time and sit with her on the sofa, I would explain to her that it was about acceptance and physical warmth – closeness. I would tell her that I did not want to see her naked, that once was more than enough. But at the time I hurt and Mum's solution to my hurt offered the best chance of pain relief I could detect.

So in went Mum and I after her. She bathed as I washed my face and brushed my teeth, only catching glimpses of her in the bathroom mirror which I was instructed to face. There was little healing to be found in that bathroom, no dulling of the pain of rejection. I left the room, eyes down to the puddles on the linoleum floor, more unsettled and even less satisfied than when I had entered.

After that experience, living with Mum and Duke became painful because I desperately wanted to be close to Mum, yet she still remained distant. I began to miss Dad as well, and Tony Royce, and Grandma ... and Mum.

My twenty days at Shaftesbury Crescent came to an end four days after my eighth birthday when Mum made an unexpected move in our relationship.

'I'm going away for a little while. I need you to go and stay with your Aunty Mary in Melbourne.'

'Where are you going, Mum?'

'I want to go to India. I need to spend some time there. I need to find myself.'

'But I thought you said that I could come with you Mum?'

'I need to go on my own first, to check that it's safe. You'll be fine with Aunty Mary. She'll look after you anyway.'

'I don't want to live with Aunty Mary. I want to be with you.'

When Barry Muir had left without taking me with him, it had led me to think that this was it. This would be how it would stay – me, Mum, and Duke by the Baseball Ground. I just hadn't seen this coming. Mum was packing all of my clothes into a brown sports bag as I cried.

'Hey, don't cry Dougie. I won't be gone forever. I'll be back soon, you'll see.'

When the taxi arrived, Mum put me in it with my brown bag. She kissed me on the cheek and gave the driver some instructions and some money. I held a note in my hand from Mum to Aunty Mary, which Mum instructed me to give her. I had stopped crying as soon as I had seen the taxi driver, as I did not want a stranger to see my tears. I waved goodbye to Mum as the taxi pulled away. Even though I could still see her through the back window of the car, she might as well have already been in India. I did not know that she would be safe. I did not know if she would go with Duke. I did not know if she would ever come back. Panic churned in my stomach as I caught sight of Mum turning her back on the street and closing the front door behind her.

The familiar and comforting journey helped me to stay calm as I left Mum, Duke, the flat, and the Baseball Ground behind me. When the taxi pulled up outside Aunt Mary's house I said thanks and got out of the car, slinging the sports bag over my shoulder. I knocked loudly on the front door as the taxi drove away. Eventually, after several knocks, Aunty Mary's shocked face appeared through her front door. She looked at me, then up the street, then down the street. Then back at me. I handed her the letter.

'Mum said to give you this.'

Aunty Mary opened the envelope and stood reading. I was waiting to give her my bag. She stopped reading as her hand dropped to her side. She looked at me again, this time with a smile.

'Well me duck, you'd better come in hadn't you?'

# 16

# MELBOURNE LOST

'Dominic abandoned by mother at Mrs Roulstone's (great aunt) house on Friday 27th April 1979 with a note asking her to care for Dominic for six months to one year approximately. Aunt unable to provide long term care – overcrowded.'

B M, Social Care Officer, 1st May 1979.

*

It had been four days since I had turned eight and with that event over, Mum was going to India without me. My mind raced with thoughts of her travelling on an aeroplane, meeting lots of Indian people, and wearing sandals again. Then my stomach rolled and plummeted when I remembered that she was going so far without me and that I would not know exactly where she was. Then my mind returned to a happy image of Mum, smiling, and 'finding herself'. I told myself that Mum would only stay in India for a couple of weeks and then she would return to get me from Melbourne. Then I looked up at Aunty Mary's face, which flickered with worry as she sat looking at the telephone. She held the letter from Mum in her hand. I wanted to read it, to see what Mum had written. I wanted to ask to see it, but I didn't.

'Aunty Mary, is my mum gonna phone?'

'Yes, duck.'

'Am I going to stay here with you, Aunty Mary?'

Aunty Mary sighed, and held her arm out in an invitation for a hug. I got up and walked into her arms. 'You are always welcome to stay with me love. We don't see enough of you anyway. It's just, well, it's just that we haven't really got enough room for you to stay here and live with us all the time. You should be with your mum anyway chuck. I don't know what she's thinking about now, all this going off to India.'

'Why is Mum phoning then?'

Hope rose inside my chest. Maybe a last minute change could mean that she would take me with her.

'She said she'd phone to check that you got here all right. At least she's got the decency to check. At least she'll know you're here and safe.'

When the phone rang, Aunty Mary let it ring twice, took a breath, and picked the hand set up.

'Hello, yes it is. Yes. He's okay Mary but...'

Aunty Mary began to frown.

'Yes, but you can't just... Mary, we haven't got enough room here. Yes I know but..."

Aunty Mary's tone suddenly changed. "You can't just leave him here Mary! Mary.... Mary, if you do I'll have to call... Mary? Mary?'

Aunty Mary put the phone down as her shoulders

slumped. Even though I could not hear what Mum had been saying, I had been caught up in the emotion of the call. My eyes welled up as I retreated further away from Aunty Mary and sat in the chair behind me. She looked at me with tear-filled eyes. Out came a hanky which she used to wipe her eyes and blow her nose, then she sniffed and said, 'Your Uncle Allan will be home soon on his motorbike. Do you want some tea, me duck?'

'Yes please, Aunty Mary.'

'Well, it's Friday! Fancy some fish and chips?'

*

The dying chokes and splutters of Uncle Allan's motorbike echoed down through the arch of the side passage and into the back garden where I had been lying on the grass and watching the clouds sail over the grey tile roof. Before he pulled the blue cover over the bike, he sat me on it and placed his round helmet on my head and tapped the top of it.

'Eee, you'll get yer own one day.'

Uncle Allen smelt of his bike – oil and petrol, and fresh air. I looked at his long sideburns as I lay my hands on the warm, creaking body of his bike. He pulled me off, put his cover on, and went into the kitchen. Soon, Aunty Mary came out.

'Are you all right playing in the garden for a bit more Dominic? I'm just finishing tea. It won't be long now.' Uncle Allan went in and closed the back door behind him.

Before bed, Aunty Mary put a hot water bottle beside me and tucked me in. Then, she reached over to the side board and took hold of a small plastic ornament of the Virgin Mary praying at the mouth of a cave. She wound it up at the base then placed it back on the dresser where it tinkled out the tune of 'Ave Maria'. Then she reached for a statue of the face of Jesus, and his praying hands. When Aunty Mary switched it on it lit up with a pale, soothing light. Although I did not know at the time, these comforting icons had been brought by Aunty Mary from a nearby Cistercian Monastery called Mount St Bernard. Aunty Mary had loved visiting this monastic community, dedicated as it was to the Virgin Mary.

'Shall we say our prayers to Jesus then?'

I nodded slowly, not quite sure of what Aunty Mary was thinking.

'Dear Lord Jesus, keep us safe as we sleep tonight. Amen.'

'Amen.'

Aunty Mary bent down and kissed me on the head. 'Sleep tight now, duck.'

I looked around the unfamiliar room. 'Can I keep Jesus on?'

'Yes, duck. We'll leave Jesus praying shall we? Don't let the bed bugs bite.'

'I won't.'

*

It was only one weekend, but that Saturday and Sunday in Melbourne are filled with bright memories. There was a pond, a haze of bluebells in a wood, and an old stately home with people parading around the lawns in fancy Victorian clothes. We visited Aunty Julie, Aunty Mary's daughter, in a flat somewhere nearby.

I loved the smells at Aunty Mary's house, both inside and out. Melbourne itself smelt fresh and mossy-sweet. The back garden smelt of flowers and cut-grass and Uncle Allan's motorbike. Inside the house smelt familiar, like old furniture, or linen. Aunty Mary had the same pomanders that Grandma used to have – white china balls with flowers painted on them and scent-holes in the top. Memories of Grandma flooded back as I sat in the front room swinging the pomander from its golden thread. Aunty Mary looked a bit like Grandma, only with darker hair and a thinner face, but her eyes were the same and the smile-lines around them. As I sat, smelling and looking at the painted flowers, I wondered if this is what Grandma had wanted – me living contently in Melbourne, with her younger sister Aunty Mary, seeing Mum perhaps, but living here. Suddenly, it all seemed to fall into place. Aunty Mary can look after me. 'It's Aunty Mary, Grandma. She can do it when you're not here anymore.'

Perhaps my Grandma had asked her sister if she would do this when she knew that she was dying. Maybe Grandma had asked Aunty Mary that day when we were waiting at the bus stop and Grandma was crying. Maybe Aunty Mary had said no. I knew it was cramped when I stayed at Aunty Mary's that weekend. Someone had to go to a friend's or sleep somewhere else so that I could stay. I do not know exactly who was living there but it felt like everyone was bending over backwards to make space for me.

Over the years I have often wondered how Aunty Mary was getting on. There were times when I had wanted to make contact with her but Mum had never been willing to give me her address. As an adult I drove through Melbourne twice, looking for Aunty Mary's house and trying to figure out exactly which street she lived in. I knocked on doors and asked bemused but very understanding residents about Aunty Mary. I couldn't even remember her surname. Some people had a vague knowledge of the family but no-one knew for sure. And then I applied for and received my records from Derby Social Services. There it all was – address, name, and dates. I sat on the information for at least two years. After an initial reading, I put them in my wardrobe and did not go back to them. There was too much to process. Finally, after another failed fishing trip in Melbourne on the way back from a conference in Bradford, it suddenly clicked. Aunty Mary's address is in my notes. I already have it.

I kicked myself for not remembering, for failing to put two and two together, and I wrote a letter. I wrote to Aunty Mary at her address in North Street in the hope that she was still there. I included my own address, my mobile number, my email address, and my Facebook account. Just in case. Just in case...

Days after posting the letter, I received a message from a stranger on Facebook. The conversation started on 12th December 2012.

Sarah: *Hi Dominic, not sure if I have the right person. But you wrote to my grandma, Mary. And I would like to get in touch with you if that's OK? Thank you.*

Dominic: *You have the right person! I guess that makes us cousins of some sort? My mum's mum was Eileen, who was your grandma's sister.*

Sarah: *Well Mary is actually my great Aunt, but because she brought up my mum I always called her grandma. My mum's mum was your mum's sister, called Ivy. I was really close to Mary. She passed away in November 1999. I have a few photos of Mary & Alan on their wedding day. My mum is Julie Bexon and she remembers you as a little boy and remembers more than me.*

Dominic: *That's really sad news, a great loss to you all. I remember visiting Julie! Wow, I am sure we will be doing lots of photo swapping! My mum, also called Mary (White), was an only child as far as I know. Her mum, Eileen, looked after me until I was 3 until she died. My mum was the self proclaimed 'black sheep' of the family, so I was not given much opportunity to connect. I found Aunty Mary's address when I got my care records recently from Derby social services. Speechless!*

Sarah: *Yea there's not a day goes by that I don't*

*think of her. I miss her so much. I'm glad you're in touch as not much family alive on Mary's side. My mum said you were such a lovely well behaved boy, very capable. Your grandma & granddad loved you so much, and she used to call you her little prince.*

Dominic: *Wow! I have one photo of my grandma, and she was kissing me on a beach! My mum did not have a great relationship with her parents, but I have really vivid and good memories of my grandma and granddad. I passed through Melbourne a couple of weeks ago, and knocked on a few doors, but I did not have the right address then. Still a sleepy place! But brought back fond memories of Mary. I seem to remember Alan having pigeons?*

Sarah: *Yea Melbourne hasn't changed much. The neighbour at the bottom of the garden (Mr Bolt) had the pigeons. My mum says do you remember your gran's dog? She thinks her name was Megan. My mum and I still live in Melbourne. I sometimes walk past Mary's house... for the memories. I have an older brother called Nick, not sure if you remember him or not.*

Dominic: *Poodle was Megan, who used to run around in circles, and big black dog called Mick. You will have to give me a low-down of the whole family. Must go for now, will send some pics of us all lots of love to you all.*

Sarah: *OK Dominic, yea that sounds good. Take care, lots of love to you & your family.*

I found myself overwhelmed afterwards. I had

family. Distant maybe, geographically and also relationally, but I had family. I had forgotten that I was my grandma's prince. As soon as I read it memories came flooding back of Grandma speaking those words of affirmation and love to me, calling me, naming me to be someone, something worthwhile. As well as the joy, there was also grief and regret. I was years too late. Aunty Mary had gone and I would never be able to meet her or speak to her about my times at her house in Melbourne. I was thirteen years too late.

I sent Sarah the very few photographs of my grandma I had, which had actually only recently come into my possession – a picture of me aged three, hugging and kissing Eileen White; Sarah's other great aunt, on a beach; Sarah said that she would talk more to her mum about me. I had at long last made contact with family in Melbourne, in the parish of Shardlow.

In April 1979, Aunty Mary did everything she could to help me. On Sunday night, she sat on the end of my bed as I snuggled into my hot water bottle. I could feel the smoothness of the cool, tight sheets on my bare feet. The praying Jesus was still casting a soft light on Aunty Mary's face as she smiled at me and rubbed my knees. Her smile faded and her face looked sad suddenly.

'We love you Dominic, and me and your Uncle Allan want what's best for you. You know that don't you now?'

'Yes.'

'Well, we've had a talk and, well, you see duck there's just not enough room here for you to stay... to live here. Well, what we..'

I sat up fast. 'Am I going back to Mum then?'

'No love, no. We don't even know where she is. She's in no fit state to look after you anyway, duck. She shouldn't have sent you here in a taxi. It's no good for you...'

'Where am I going then?'

'Well, me and Uncle Allan have decided that we will ring Social Services tomorrow and...'

'Why can't I stay here with you though?'

'You can come and visit us, duck. We'd love to see more of you. There just isn't any room here at the moment.'

'Will I go back to The Mount?'

'The what? The Mount? Well. I'm not really sure. We'll have to see what they say tomorrow.'

'Can't I just stay for one more day Aunty Mary? Can't you phone them on Tuesday?'

Aunty Mary looked at me with shiny eyes. 'We'll see love. Anyway, you don't need to worry about it. Everything will come out in the wash. You'll see.' She shuffled up the bed towards me and gave me a hug and kissed my cheek. 'It will all work out for the best I'm sure.'

As I lay in the bed looking at the hands of Jesus, trying to get to sleep, my mind raced and tears rolled onto my pillow. Despite the gentle glow of Jesus and his hands, the room looked dark and I couldn't see what was in the corners. I closed my eyes and pulled the top of the covers over my head.

*

I knew Aunty Mary loved me. Even Uncle Allan, I knew, loved me. But I knew that they could not have me to stay. As Monday ran out and Tuesday got closer, a new worry gripped me, one that I had never been bothered by before.

'Aunty Mary, if I move, then how will Mum know where to get me from when she comes back?'

Even though I was reassured that they would tell her where I was, I did not feel totally safe with the arrangement. I might be put somewhere that Aunty Mary didn't know about. How would Mum ever find me if I moved now? She thought that I was staying in Melbourne until she got back. How would my mum know that I had moved?

'Can we phone Mum and tell her where I'm going to Aunty Mary?'

'No, duck. We haven't even got a number. Don't you worry yourself now. I will make sure that we tell her where you are when the time comes.'

When Barry turned up on Tuesday morning, I repacked my clothes into my brown sports bag and sat in the living room watching Barry and Aunty Mary talk. I looked at the smooth round pomander on the sideboard. When the time came, I hugged Aunty Mary and climbed into Barry's car.

'Well then Dominic, off we go then, eh?'

'Am I going back to The Mount then?'

That was the obvious choice. I imagined myself seeing the boys again and Tony Royce. I pictured the car pulling up on the slope of the drive, me getting out and giving Tony Royce a hug, and being made a fuss of by everyone. I was suddenly nervous about seeing everyone again. Barry looked at me.

'It won't be The Mount Dominic. That would be a bit like taking a step backwards, wouldn't it?'

'No, it wouldn't. I like it at The Mount. Where am I going then?'

'Well, I think you'll like it. I've managed to arrange a place for you at Birdcage Walk.'

As the car engine chugged to life and we rolled away down country lanes and past rivers and fields, I imagined a small budgie in a cage. The idea of going to a birdcage did not rest easily on my mind. As we broke into the traffic and buildings of Derby, I felt heavy. I had a faraway feeling inside – faraway from everywhere I wanted to be and everyone I wanted to be with. And so began my days at my fourth children's home in Derby, in Birdcage Walk.

# 17

# UNCLE TOM'S GARDEN

'Little anxiety was shown when Dominic was admitted to Birdcage Walk. He is becoming conditioned to being received into care. He has also mentioned that his mother may be at a café on St Thomas Road, which I am aware is frequented by prostitutes. His acceptance of his mother's rejection is very sad although he remains loyal to her, having told me of the café saying I must not tell anyone.'

B M Social Worker, 1st May 1979.

'On 3rd July 1979 Mr Swainson came into the Office. He is a registered drug addict and has been sharing part of Mary's last address. He stated that Mary had continued to live at that address until 29th June 1979, when she had finally left, leaving no forwarding address.'

*

It was a crisp, fresh morning as I sat in my parked car looking up the hill. Coming back after all these years felt like returning to a movie that had been left on pause and forgotten. As I stared at the hill over my dashboard I remembered that on Saturday mornings I used to receive my pocket money and then I would trundle up and over that hill to the shop beyond. I would buy a Mars Bar, or a Twix, and a Whizzer and Chips comic. The hill was also the way to school, to Reigate Juniors where I had to wear grey shorts and a stripy tie. I had built a rocket ship out of cereal and egg boxes at Reigate Juniors and loved to run around the huge, grass playing field at break times.

I locked the car then walked up the pavement a little to find the familiar entrance to the walk. I turned into it between the green hedges on either side which, unlike in 1979, I could now see over. To my right I passed a new building where an old scout hut used to be. I had been to Scouts once or twice but did not like the Scout Leader. A memory of me and another boy fighting with each other and falling into the bush on the opposite side came flooding back. Ahead of me stood the same concrete bollard in the middle of the walk which I used to leapfrog on the way to school. Further ahead was the field in which I would play football with my friends, the grass still glistening in the morning dew. On I went, past the hedges, and there it was to my right – Birdcage Walk. A new fence stood at the border of the front garden where there had been none. The path, newly paved but still at the same sharp angle from the walk, led up to the front door.

I knocked, and waited, then knocked again. No-one answered. On the wall near the door there was an organisational plaque, telling me what the building was now used for – no longer a children's home, but still used to help people who needed support. I wanted to go in and look around, to see the long front room with the wooden floor and blue sofas. I wanted to go upstairs and see my bedroom where I had snuggled with my black-and-white Panda Bear and read 'Walter the Lazy Mouse'. When I had arrived at Birdcage Walk, I was presented with a bag taken from the attic and invited to rummage and choose one teddy bear which would be mine to keep. Panda Bear was small and black-and-white; eventually he became just as loved as Pink Panther had been, who sadly had by then long gone.

I was also invited to choose one book from the shelf which would be mine to keep. I was drawn to a picture of a happy mouse on the front cover, reclining in the wheat while frogs frolicked in the water beyond. The story, which I read over and over again, was about a mouse called Walter who was too slow in life and who eventually became forgotten by his family and left behind. Some kind and funny frogs took him in and cared for him. Eventually Walter said goodbye to the frogs because he wasn't a frog. He was a mouse who found his family again. I had felt like Walter with the frogs when I lived at Birdcage Walk for a year and four months and I knew that, like him, my mum would remember me and come back for me.

I wanted to see the bed where Uncle Tom and

Aunty Katy had kissed me goodnight and tucked in my bedcovers. Uncle Tom had to stoop low with his tickly moustache to kiss me on the forehead. Aunty Katy would jump on the bed and tickle me in a cloud of her sweet perfume and then cover my face with her long brown curls as she gave me a big goodnight smacker on the lips. I wanted to see my bedside table where I placed my Walter book at night and on top of which I would place the buzzer attached to the metal gauze under my sheet. When it went off in the middle of the night like a siren, the nocturnal bed patrol would swoop in and whisk me to the bathroom for a cold flannel wash and then march me back to my bed so I could help them take off the wet sheets and remake the bed. I am not sure which therapeutic aid helped me to stop wetting the bed the most – the moisture alarm, or the inhumane treatment at the hands of the grumpy night staff.

There was still no answer at the door, not even a flicker of a curtain. It was a Sunday, clearly a day off for the team who now worked in the house. I crept around to the side, peering into the kitchen through the glass side door. It looked different, yet familiar enough to cause a flood of kitchen memories to pour into my mind like warm custard: the round old lady who used to let me open cans on the huge metal contraption bolted to the wall; the enormous white fridge from which I was allowed to take the jug of cold custard and eat the hard skin on the top.

I then peered over the white wooden fence into

that garden – that garden, where I had laid on my back and watched a thousand white clouds sailing overhead through the blue sky, driven by winds high up; that grass, which had risen softly to meet me as my hero, an older peer, had knocked me out in a gloved boxing match; that tree under which I had tried to bury my ill-fitting school shoes, the ones I hated because my socks kept slipping down the backs. I wanted to leap over the fence and run around like I used to. I would have dug and searched in the mud and dust by the path to see if any of my plastic soldiers were still lying buried. I stopped myself from leaping over ... just.

Stepping back I took another look at the front of the house. This house had been my home for nearly a year-and-a-half, from 1st May 1979 to 26th September 1980. From age eight to age nine-and-a-half, the frontage of this house had greeted me after days out in the sun, rain and snow. All the staff, who we called uncles and aunts, had looked after me and nurtured me, a little like Walter's foster-frogs.

On up the path I walked, past small houses and the football field, which also looked a lot smaller than it used to. I remembered running from it and into the house, hot and thirsty, and being presented with a big glass of water, or squash, or milk. Further up and across I spotted the sloped streets which had iced over in the deep of winter providing me with paths to slip and slide down. Then I doubled back, with one last glance at the house as I walked by. I imagined the back dining room where we would eat pies and veg and all sorts of wonderful food. It was also the room in which I had been presented with my special presents for managing to achieve nocturnal dryness at last, after months of not so gentle encouragement from the night staff. I had played with the foot-tall Darth Vader and the Tie-Fighter with detachable wings for days.

This time I did not go past the bollard in the middle of the walk. I scanned behind briefly to check for onlookers, then I trotted up to it and scaled it with a small leap – much less effort now than when I had been four-and-a-half feet tall. Before me lay the ongoing Green of Birdcage Walk over the street, flanked by houses on either side. The boy who had knocked me out in a play fight had taught me how to knock on people's doors and run away in this very Green. He had also taught me about punk rock, and anarchy – an 'A' in a circle that he drew in a black marker-pen anywhere he could. He also educated me as to why I shouldn't like the Queen, or the 'Government', which I didn't really know a great deal about anyway.

One day we had walked through this Green together, swearing loudly for fun and singing brash songs together, and we had simply carried on walking. We made it together to his relative's house near the Rolls Royce factory, then to his mother's caravan in a field. We hid together from the police in dark gardens and under caravan seats. Having eventually been found by the police, I had spent a night alone in a cell before being returned to

Birdcage Walk. Adam was my hero, with his blonde skinhead hair cut and his clean punch.

Sitting again in my car, I set my mind to the next task in hand. I had already visited The Mount on Albany Road, which was now a private dwelling undergoing extensive renovation. Even that garden, which had seemed absolutely huge as a child, looked small as I peered over the wall through the sprouting buddleia. As I drove away from Birdcage Walk, I began to feel the excitement of my next adventure as I set off towards the centre of Derby to find Martin Street and St Wurburgh's Church – and any trace of a man called Harry Cristos, the son of a Greek-Cypriot restauranteur.

*

Life at Birdcage Walk had been good despite the misleading name. I thought about Mum most at night as I lay alone in the dark and least when I was adventuring or misbehaving anarchically with Adam. It took me a while to warm up to all my new 'uncles' and 'aunts', but clear favourites emerged in good time. At first there was an older lady who used to hug me and feed me lots. She was the one who used to let me raid the fridge for cold custard skin. She retired half way through my stay but was soon and easily replaced by Aunty Katy. She was bouncy, dungareed, and betrothed to someone who wasn't me, which I was unhappy about. I danced with her at her wedding with my feet dangling as she pretended that I was just as tall as her. It is fair to say that Aunty Katy was my first crush. She was just too kind and happy and smelt far too nice.

Then there was Uncle Tom. Uncle Tom was tall and thin with a mop of curly hair and a bushy moustache under his nose. Always cracking a joke or lightening the mood, he was a fun person to be with. He had a band that played 'experimental rock music' and he was as cool as anyone I knew. I had sat with Uncle Tom and watched sinister lines of marching hammers on telly, accompanied by classes of angry children telling their teacher to 'leave those kids alone.' I felt the emotion with Uncle Tom as the teachers were told 'All in all, you're just another brick in the wall'. Uncle Tom played in on a 'synth' and wanted to become a rock star one day.

He was the one who bought my Darth Vader and Tie-Fighter presents. He was the one who encouraged me to play goalie in the school football team and helped me to practice in the back garden. Uncle Tom was the one who came to see me perform as the Sun in my Ballet Sun Ray dance in front of the Mayor of Derby. I was the only boy in my Ballet class so was the natural choice for the star role of 'The Sun,' while all the girls, or 'sun-rays', ran around me in circles. Even now I can remember some of the positions and the spins and leaps. Uncle Tom once told me, 'You've got really good balance and you're very strong. You could be a ballet dancer or a football player, whatever you want to be.'

Uncle Tom wanted me to live with him. Barry, my social worker, sat with me and explained the situation as best he could. I almost leapt when he told me that Uncle Tom wanted me to visit his home to meet his family. The excitement was soon tempered however by the realisation that if I lived with Uncle Tom, Mum would have two moves to catch up with when she came back to find me.

*

When I stepped out of Barry's car into the street on which Uncle Tom lived, I immediately recognised it. High up in a roof, over the road from Uncle Tom's house, was the attic room where I had first smoked weed from a watery glass jar with Mum. I suddenly wondered if Uncle Tom knew the men who had been kind enough and actually looked a lot like Uncle Tom in appearance. Two worlds collided in that street for me that day and suddenly I could see potential for common ground between them.

It felt strange entering the private life of a member of staff, albeit my favourite one, who normally left the boundaries of my life after a shift and disappeared into the mystery of his own life, his own family. Suddenly, here I was on hallowed ground, stepping into the mystery. Barry and Uncle Tom led me through the house into the kitchen at the back. Mrs Uncle Tom put out her hands and offered me a hug, which I accepted in a stiff sort of way. She was pretty and smiled at me. I stood and looked around the small kitchen at the sink and the washing up in it, the tiles on the floor, and the shafts of golden sunlight breaking through the back window, trying to imagine it as mine – as my kitchen, with my foster parents.

The back door suddenly flew open and in fell a girl and a boy, both just a little younger than me. The boy smiled at me then ran past into the house. The girl stood watching me, and held her dad's hand.

'Why don't you go with Millie and play in the garden Dom? There's a swing at the back and some rabbits. Millie, go and show Dominic the rabbits will you?' Uncle Tom beamed at me from behind his moustache and put his hand on my shoulder. I could see Uncle Tom's garden through the kitchen window. It was green and bright. It was a long garden which had a slope going up at the very back, with a swing clearly visible at the foot of the slope. It looked warm and exciting. It was yet another private mystery to be explored. Millie looked at me, smiled and held out her hand towards me. The boy dashed in from behind me carrying a plastic toy and bumped her hand out of the way as he raced through the door back into the garden. Millie again raised her hand towards me, fingers outstretched. I smiled but my hand wavered at my side. Then it dropped.

'No thanks.'

I looked up at Barry, hoping he would help me resist the urge to reach out and grab hold of her hand and run into the garden to swing, and play, and have fun with Uncle Tom's family.

'Go on then, go and see what's in the garden, Dominic. Go on, it looks nice and warm out there.'

Still I stood, eyes to the tiles, feet rooted to the spot. Suddenly I wanted to leave. How could I ever live with Uncle Tom and his family? How could I ever betray Mum like this? If she came back searching for me it would be bad enough that I was in care, in a children's home, instead of being at Aunty Mary's house where she sent me. I could imagine her on Uncle Tom's doorstep shouting and crying, swearing at him and telling him to give her son back to her. I could imagine leaving Uncle Tom's house with Mum, feeling like I had betrayed both of them.

Then I looked back at the girl and the garden through the window and I just wished it wasn't all so complicated. I wanted to reach out and meet her fingers in mid air, to feel the physical substance of the opportunity she was offering to me. There she was, a young girl who had never met me before, offering me space in her garden, in her family. My hand wavered again, then reattached itself firmly and flatly to my side.

'No thanks. I want to stay in here with you.'

The girl's smile collapsed into disappointment as she clung to her daddy's brown corduroy trousers. 'OK Millie, you go and play. He might come out in a minute or two.'

I never stepped into Uncle Tom's garden. If I could relive that moment I would grab Millie's hand with both of mine, saving her the disappointment and rejection. I would run into the garden and swing and play and run and laugh. I would grasp the opportunity with both hands and never let go. I would live with Uncle Tom and his family and enjoy endless summer days in his garden, living under his roof. But I didn't. I couldn't. There was too much at stake and I had somehow to stay strong.

*

One day Uncle Tom sat with me in the living room and explained that he had something important to tell me. He put his hand on my shoulder and looked into my eyes. Maybe he was about to tell me that he was going to foster me anyway, even though I had said that I didn't want him to. Maybe he was about to take away the burden of my decision and decide for me. Part of me began to anticipate falling into a safer place, a more peaceful predicament where choice was no longer mine to make and uphold. He was going to take me anyway just because he wanted me.

'Dominic, I'm going to be leaving Birdcage Walk for good soon.'

My heart plummeted. I could have wailed. Instead I sat silently, trying my absolute best not to look shocked.

'I'm not leaving straightaway but I've decided to spend more time working with the band and writing music. I'll still come back and visit you, even after I've left. You okay with that? I mean, would you like me to visit you?'

'Yes.'

'Aunty Katy will take over as your key worker. Would that be okay? I know you get on well with her as well, eh?'

'Yes.'

I couldn't say much more without my bottom lip starting to quiver so I kept quiet. After the conversation on the sofa, after doing my best to smile and look happy, I went into the toilet and cried big, rolling tears, as silently as I could.

One evening, Uncle Tom brought his band to Birdcage Walk and set up in the living room. On came the disco lights as Uncle Tom played his synthesiser while his band mates strummed and rocked out on their guitars. I sat back on the sofa and watched in awe as Uncle Tom danced around behind his synthesiser, pulling funny faces on the loudest notes. His 'experimental rock music' washed over me in pleasant waves as my wide eyes feasted on the visual delights.

There must have been other people watching that night, perhaps sitting beside me on the sofa, but I can't remember anyone else being there. It was just me, Uncle Tom and his band. The whole performance was for my benefit and Uncle Tom's eyes, at least when he wasn't looking where he was putting his fingers, were locked on me.

If I ever find Uncle Tom, I will tell him how special that performance was for me. I will sit with him in his house and talk to him. I will explain why I couldn't go into his garden in 1980 but how much I wanted to as well. If he still has a garden I will go into it with him this time. I will step out of Uncle Tom's kitchen and into his sun-drenched garden of delights.

# 18

# THE CAT LADY OF NOTTINGHAM

'I would strongly recommend that parental rights be assumed under Section 2 (1) of the Children Act 1948, on the grounds that his mother has so consistently failed without reasonable cause to discharge the obligations of parent as to be unfit to have the care of the child.'

J.F. G, South-West Area Officer (8th August 1979).

'Dominic has settled extremely well at 'Birdcage' and has made many friends although it is noticeable that he does not like close contact and tends to keep relationships at a fairly superficial level, no doubt his own attempt to see that he does not get hurt again in the future. He has also stated to me that he much prefers to remain at Birdcage Walk than to return home to his mother, should the opportunity present itself.'

B M, Social Worker (8th August 1979).

'Dominic talks more frequently about his life with

his mother. He refuses fostering, but stated that if his mother would turn up he would go with her. He likes swimming and athletics and expresses a wish to join a club to pursue these activities.'

Mrs E S, Head of House (19th November 1979).

*

I sat alone on the garden bench in the cold shade, silently waiting for her. Two letters had arrived from Mum, the first in February 1980, the second in March 1980. It was now 23rd April and my ninth birthday.

Both letters sat in my back pocket dog-eared and frayed on the creases. My legs swung backwards and forwards rhythmically as my toes scraped on the concrete. Any minute now Mum would walk out of the back door into the sunlit garden and I would see her with my own eyes. I did not quite know what to expect. I could not pin the situation down in my mind, could not exactly imagine how she would be, how I would be. The sunlight had just started to fade making it chilly in the shade.

Mum had written that she had needed an operation to remove some stones; that she was recovering; that a Jamaican man called Eli was looking after her; that she lived in a flat in a house in Nottingham near Nottingham Castle and she wanted me to visit her. Mum had written that she would soon be going to Jamaica with Eli for six weeks, after which she would return to get me. She wanted me to be with her, to go to Jamaica with her and Eli.

It was India all over again. I had so wanted to travel to India with Mum, to feel the warmth of the sun and eat curry and chapatti every day, to see the colours and the beautiful Indian people – the women with silky hair and men with grey beards and kind smiles. I had wanted to be with Mum when she 'found herself' in India. I had wanted to find myself too in India.

Now Jamaica threatened to take Mum away again. Weeks in Melbourne had turned into a year in 'Birdcage', where aunts and uncles and Social Workers talked about fostering and section twos and asked me, 'what do you want? What do you want?' How long would Jamaica be? Six weeks? Six months? Six years?

Aunty Mary and her daughter Julie loved on me when I went to Melbourne and Hinkley. Uncle Tom and Aunty Katy hugged me and joked with me and shared the highs and lows of life with me. What do you want? What do you want? What... do... you... want? I knew what I wanted but it changed from moment to moment. I wanted everything, then nothing. I knew I didn't want this, sitting in a cold shadow waiting for the only person who I could not help but need, who would know that I had almost betrayed her.

Mum suddenly appeared with a football and a small present in her hands. I stood quickly but stopped myself from leaping up. She dropped the ball which bounced and rolled away as she threw her arms out towards me. My hands rose with my elbows pinned to my ribs as I turned my head sideways, presenting Mum with a board of a boy to hug. It's not that I had decided to hold back; it's just that when it came to it, after a year's absence and silence, I did. Mum stood back and took stock of me, her smile beaming and melting my ice.

'Dougie, Dougie. You've grown so much... look at you. Oh Dougie, it's so good to see you. I've missed you so much.'

'I've missed you too Mum.'

'Aw, I know you have. Happy birthday son.'

'Thanks. I'm nine now.'

'Yes I know, I know... I'm sorry Dougie. I'm so sorry that I left you and...'

Mum began to cry and hugged me again. She wiped her tears away as I held mine in. If I pressed my back teeth together hard, the tears remained behind my eyes and facial muscular contortion was kept at bay.

'Have you had your operation?'

'Yes, yes... it's all done now. I've got a scar and it's still healing, but I'm fine. The doctor says I've got to watch what I eat... to cut out the fatty foods like chips and... Did you get my letters then?'

'Yes, I got two of your letters.'

'So what are you doing now? They told me you like football. I brought you a football... where is it?'

Mum scanned the ground and picked up the ball,

handing it to me. 'Here, it's for you.'

'Thanks Mum.'

The ball had black-and-white hexagonal patches and smelt new. For some reason this object, the feel of it, the smell of it, was filled with emotion more than air. Even to this day, there is something about a brand new football for me.

'And this... this is for you as well. Here, open it.'

Mum presented me with the square present wrapped in football paper. I took it and pulled off the paper, revealing a blue plastic box. I opened the box with a creaking sound. A smile snuck across my face as I saw the wrist watch inside sitting on its stand – a watch, ticking and shiny. I had never had my own wrist watch.

'Do you like it?'

'Yes Mum, I really like it.' Mum grasped the box and took the watch off the stand and then we fumbled for a while trying to get it onto my wrist.

'There. You can tell everyone the time now. It looks so smart Dougie. My son, my son.'

'Thanks Mum.'

I had coped well with the football as I had seen it early, but the watch caught me off guard. It was something she had thought about. It was something she had taken a chance on me liking. And she had got it right.

We sat on the bench together and conversation ebbed and flowed around ballet, and Melbourne, eventually turning to Jamaica.

'I want you to come with me. These people are

trying to take you away from me, but I want you to come with me.' The corners of Mum's mouth turned down as she said 'these people', and her eyes darted towards the house.

'I need to go there to check it out for us first. It's a long way away and I want to make sure it's safe for you. Will you come with me?'

'Mmm.' I nodded with my eyes down.

Now I felt the tears burning behind my eyes and my teeth clenched hard.

'I'll make sure everything is okay and then I'll come back for you. You'll see. I'll come back for you, Dougie, my son. I'm so proud of you.'

After Mum had left, I felt like a caged animal. Suddenly the whole world was uncomfortable. Nothing felt right or safe; not this side of the room, nor that side; not being away from Mum, or being with her.

What do you want?

What ... do ... you ... want?

*

'Dominic has shown considerable progress at Birdcage Walk in his ability to accept and show affection and preparedness to display emotion. However, he is a child who bottles his worries and feelings up and he displays a good deal of strength in his capacity to carry his troubles with him. Whilst progress in breaking down these barriers has been made the reappearance of his mother has seemed to have arrested this development.'

B M, Social Worker (8th May 1980).

*

Not long afterwards I was allowed to visit Mum in Nottingham, under the watchful eye of Mr Muir, the social worker.

I entered her lair with trepidation, like a mouse creeping into a cat's basket, delighted by the sight of her subtle smile below deep green eyes yet wary of her sheathed claws. My shabby brown sports bag was laid before her as tribute, and a subtle sign to her that I had not forgotten our past encounters.

'Let it be known between us that I am here with hope and caution in equal measure, and that I will not be your prey tonight.'

The Cat Lady hugged me, naming me once again 'Dougie', and pulling me into the soft, cool folds of her kaftan. My advocate and protector Mr Muir lurked behind me, supposedly ready to fight should he judge that the need arise.

As I inhaled Mum's white musk perfume, I let my face rest, if a little stiffly, on her chest and I became all but lost as she pulled me in. There I stood, melting and swaying in Mum's rocking grasp. The presence of Mr Muir became a token one and when he left, I was glad. An intoxicating haze of incense enveloped me as I stepped into the lounge. I could see silks on the walls through the joss stick haze, embroidered with sequins and mirrors and elephants. I sank back into the soft settee, relieved.

Before me was a low table surfaced with brown patterned tiles, on which was placed a green earthenware mug full of steamy sweet tea. Above my head hung a large glass-framed picture of a man's billowing face with protruding lips, like the unfurled sail of a ship, propped up on sticks in a far away desert. Peace and contentment washed over me as I sat watching Mum swish back into the room from the kitchen holding a green plate filled with chocolaty animal-shaped biscuits.

And then she sat next to me, close enough to hold on to. She looked at me with clear eyes and a natural smile. She touched my hand and held it. I sat looking at her eyes, pushing the animals one by one into my teeth, showering crumbs down upon my jumper. She spoke softly with gentle squeezes of my hand as her melodious words and laughter babbled over me like a gentle flow of water. As the light dimmed, she disappeared again into the kitchen as her soft and fury accomplice pounced upon my lap and sat, purring, padding its claws into my leg.

Mum said that I could go out and play for a little while so long as I didn't go beyond where she could see me from the window. She told me not to talk to anyone and to be back in before it was dark.

I left the flat in the large Victorian house and walked down the curvy pathway under the window, smiling at but not talking to the ladies who were standing beneath the lamppost. They looked like how Mum used to look, all dressed up. I thought about Mum and how different she looked today, like her old self. She smelt right, sounded right. Even her flat, although not Martin Street, felt like home. It had nice furniture and earthenware and candles and sweet smoke. There were sparkly things glinting on the walls like fairy fires. There was no-one else. It was just Mum and I, and her soft, resonant cat. The kitchen smelt of cat and cat food, just like a kitchen should. I had all of her attention, all of her love. She hugged me and touched me and let me into her previously impenetrable space. At last I was in once again. I had access to closeness and warmth, to nurture and inner peace. My mum was not like these ladies who smiled at me as I raced back up the hill as the streetlights flickered on.

I came back to the pungent smell of cheese on toast, browned under the grill and smothered in tomato ketchup. After tea I sank into a hot bubble bath to the distant sound of Mum strumming her guitar in the lounge. Steam hung in the air of the bathroom like a rainforest mist as I sank underneath the green-tinged Radox water like a crocodile.

Later we sat and watched a black-and-white Dracula film together as Mum smoked and puffed away. We relaxed on the soft sofa under the desert-bound face above us. When it was time for bed, Mum took hold of my brown sports bag and my hand and led me to a room which had been prepared for me. She sat on my bed and helped me to unpack my bag, placing T-shirts and underwear in drawers and trousers in the wardrobe. When the cat jumped onto my bed she sat and stroked it, talking to me.

She kissed me on the cheek and pushed my brown sports bag up high onto the top of the wardrobe, as if it were no longer needed. She left me with the cat on my bed and explained that the lights creeping through my curtains were the spotlights illuminating the walls of Nottingham Castle. The cat nudged my hand with his wet nose every time I stopped stroking him and he purred and purred, until I finally drifted off to sleep.

Meanwhile the Cat Lady purred in contentment at the timely return of her only son. She sat and smiled, giving a slow blink of her green, feline eyes which shone in the dark.

*

'Miss White resumed contact with this office on 23rd April 1980, and there have been regular contacts between Mary and myself since then. I served her with a notification of the Sub-Committee's Resolution and she immediately lodged an appeal.

It appears that during the last twelve months a relationship has developed between Mary and Eli, a person she has known for a number of years and who is known to Dominic. They are now cohabiting as man and wife and Mary is expecting a baby in December. During the past four months I have endeavoured to develop a working relationship with Mary, and to clarify in my own mind where Dominic's future lies.

Dominic wishes to return home to his mother, and from my conversations with her Mary is determined to maintain her rights as a parent and to have Dominic back with her. She has expressed a definite unwillingness to accept the parental rights assumption, but equally has said that she will not attend a Court Hearing for the appeal. Whilst at first sight this might appear to be an ambivalent stance, and one that is difficult to understand or accept, it becomes more understandable when Mary's social background is taken into account and her difficulties in coping with agencies such as ourselves.

I have considered at length what action we should take with regard to this appeal hearing, and have discussed it with my colleagues at the Area Office. On the one hand, since parental rights were assumed only a year ago it might seem logical to oppose Miss White's appeal, since many of the reasons for seeking the resolution in the first place might appear to remain valid although only in an historic perspective. The present situation is somewhat different than a year ago however, since Mary is presenting as somewhat more mature. She has a steady, stable relationship, she is expecting a further child and I am of the opinion that if rehabilitation is possible for Dominic now, or in the next year or so, it is the most appropriate time. Whilst I recognise that a parental rights assumption does not preclude us from placing Dominic back home with his mother, any attempts by us to fight Mary in the Courts would I am fairly certain jeopardise any chances of cooperation between us, and therefore tarnish any negotiations we wish to make in the future regarding Dominic's well being.

I therefore suggest to your Worships that we do not oppose Miss White's appeal against the assumption of parental rights under Section II of the 1948 Act.'

B C, Report for Derby Juvenile Court, 26th September 1980.

# 19

# JAMAICAN KUNG FU

Saying goodbye to the uncles and aunts of Birdcage Walk was a big emotional wrench, especially when Aunty Katy cried and made me promise to write a letter as soon as I got to Jamaica and then to keep in touch. She pushed a note into my hand as she sniffed and snivelled.

'Here, this is the address just in case you forget it. Don't forget, I want a letter. You hear me?'

'Yes.'

I did write her a letter, on blue airmail paper with white and red striped edges. The only bit of it I can remember was: 'Dear Aunty Katy, I have arrived safely, and it is very hot.'

On our journey to Jamaica I fought aliens and mutants in my head. Mum bought me my first ever *2000AD* comic at the airport which I devoured on the huge Boeing 747, also known by the nickname Queen of the skies. Once she had finished with her book, I got to feast my eyes on that as well. It was a full colour photo story of cinematic stills from the first *Alien* film. Most memorable of all the images were the pale face-hugger, the stomach-ripping worm bursting through John Hurt's white T-shirt, and the slick, darkly armoured, brain-biting xenomorph alien. It was either that or the in-flight movie, Kramer Vs Kramer. Not for me thanks. From the pages of *2000AD*, Judge Dredd was a revelation, as was Slaine, Strontium Dog and Rogue Trooper. This was a journey into Mum's taste in sci-fi, which she willingly shared with me. As the sea sparkled with sunlight-crested waves below, I sat beside her using courage, skill and futuristic military hardware to combat the enemies of goodness and peace.

One of the first movies I watched in Jamaica happened to be *The Harder They Come* starring Jimmy Cliff, who professed that 'the harder they come, the harder they fall, one and all', before providing a demonstration of this principle by slashing his bicycle-stealing enemy across the face with a paring knife. This film was too violent for Mum who refused to watch it. It was just as well that Mum's favourite pastime on a Friday evening was drinking white rum with Eli in the bars of Yallahs Bay instead of going where I went. Every Friday night was Kung Fu cinema for a dollar which afforded a seat on a low gym bench which formed the front row. Me, flanked by my best friends Robert and Pepito, sat wide-eyed drinking 20 cent pop in front of a hoard of boys and men swigging Dragon Stout or Redstripe Beer behind us. Our bodies swayed as our hands shadowed the Kung Fu moves flickering before us as the kinetic action danced on the white wall. Mantis, Snake, Monkey, The Iron Fist. Film after film by the Shaw Brothers was cranked out week after week on the temperamental projector in the middle-back of the hot, smoky room. Emotional literacy lessons in love, hate, revenge and courage were taught by masters and pupils who flicked their plaited braids tidily around their necks before they fought their enemies bloodily to the death. Shouts of 'Woiiiii' and 'Raaaas' would roll over me like waves as the heroes performed the art of combat with enduring bravery. For me it was a continuation of an emotional coming of age started a long time ago in a galaxy far, far away, and now furthered amidst forests of swaying giant bamboo, jade palaces and Shoalin temples.

We never merely walked from the picture house to the bars in Yallahs Bay; we always leaped and fought our way there in the styles of Crane, Dragon Fist and Tiger-Claw. By the time we found Mum and Eli they were usually merry from rum and ale, and far more likely to treat us to a piece of jerk chicken each, plucked from the intoxicating plumes of smoke which bellowed from the fire-filled barrels along the roadside. We pestered, scored fire-scorched chicken, collected beer bottle tops to harvest the rubber stoppers inside which we used as gambling currency, and then fought more epic battles with hands covered in sweet jerk sauce on the way back up the stone track to Granny's house.

Mum and Eli eventually strolled up behind us smoking and swaying to the music playing on the stereo. Is this Love? Is this love? Is this love? Is this love they are feeling? Then I would stand under the star-sprinkled sky with Mum, counting shooting stars. That sky, ripped in half by the silver-bright ribbon of the Milky Way, was truly amazing, night after night. The crickets trilled a chorus as Granny sat shelling gungo peas on the veranda in a haze of smoke pouring from the anti-mosquito bucket burning on the floor.

Even the nights were hot in Jamaica. When I first stepped out of the Air Canada Jet from Miami, in the dark of a Kingston night, I felt that there was no air to breathe. It made me panic at first, bringing on the urge to retreat into the air-conditioned jet behind me. I was so tired by the time the taxi arrived at Granny's house on that first night that climbing into a double bed with three strangers already sleeping in it felt quite okay. I was just glad that I got my own pillow. Granny, a warm, round Jamaican duchess, handed me the pillow. 'Dis-a your pillow now Dominic. Keep a hold of it. G'wan now an' sleep. You mus be very tired affa dat lang, lang journey.'

In the morning, the man on the radio told me that it was eighty two degrees in the shade. As the day warmed up into a searing heat, I realised why the distinction between in and out of shade was so important. Catching a breeze was far more soothing than sitting in the mostly airless shade, so down to the beach we all went – down the sloping white stone path, past the hut which sold Milo bedtime drink and bottles of Supermalt, and past the happy boat builders working on hulls with their iron tools on the edge of the beach.

Underneath the surface of the warm Caribbean sea was a hiding place from the sun and a world of fun and adventure. Children by the dozens frolicked and splashed around me, boys pushing, pulling and tossing me into the air, and girls giggling at me and splashing me from a safe distance. Mum swam like a frog while we all took it in turns to ride on her neck behind her, while Eli unnerved the whole lot of us by disappearing under the gentle waves and pulling his randomly chosen victim under the water unexpectedly. Then we would run on the sand and as the days and weeks passed, under the tutelage of the Kung Fu masters, we would fight and fight and fight, augmenting our kinetic action by vocalising swishing sounds as our steel palms forged their way through the air.

It was like Mum was the mother of all of these children, and me. Her name was called over and over. Her attention was begged whilst she bobbed in the waves. I joined in, happy to share Mum's attention with all of my newfound friends, who to the last were kind-hearted and full of fun. When Mum did single me out, when she bent her focus towards me, it felt rich and lavish. When she tracked me on the beach from behind her camera, clicking and smiling in her flowing sarong, I beamed my love back, and played to the lens – a mop of unkempt hair, golden-brown skin, bent knees, arms crossed with hands as flat as the lethal chopping blades they had become.

'Smile Dougie. Ha, no, that's a serious, fighting

face. Go on, crack me a smile.'

Click.

Captured in the shining moment.

One to keep forever, to remind me of just how good life can get.

One to put in the back pocket of my jeans.

On the way back we stopped at the standpipe shower under the loofah tree to wash the salt from our skin and swimwear.

'Make sure you wash your sandals out as well Dougie. If you keep washing the salt water out they will last longer. They won't rot away.'

They were my Jamaican sandals – brown leather, open-toed, comfy beyond description, and precious to me. I was the only kid around Granny's house who owned a pair.

Then after the shower, past the boat builders again and back up the hill to Granny's house. By the time we reached home, after sucking our triangle black grape ice pops, we were just as hot as when we had set off for the beach.

The fact that I had white, well, golden brown skin, made me stand out from the crowd. I was so easy to spot from a distance. On the half hour trek to school the Rasta-men smoking along the blue wall on the edge of Yallahs town would shout after me 'Wah 'gwan coolie bwoy?'

My friend Robert often accompanied us, the younger children, to school although he himself did not attend. He was in his early teens and was self-educated in the school of life. I called him Robert because that was his name and I wanted him to know that I liked his name. Most other people, however, called him Big Rat. Eventually, I asked him about this.

'Robert, why does everyone call you Big Rat?'

'Some a dem think I is a rat. Always slinkin around looking fi food an ting.'

'So do you get fed at home then?'

'Usually, yes. Money a tight sometimes though. Ya know a-wah me-a say?'

'Uh-hu.'

'Why do they call me 'coolie bwoy' Robert? What's a 'coolie bwoy'?'

Robert laughed, holding his sides and bending his tall wiry frame over me.

'You neva know what a coolie is? To raaaaas! Mek I tell you den.' He took my arm in his big hand and pointed to my skin. 'Dis is a coolie bwoy. Dis here white skin. Des a whole heap a coolie people from dar India. Dem come over to cut de sugar cane, but now dem part a di island. Mek dem think you is a coolie bwoy. To raaaaas!'

Robert became my best friend, my island guide, and my protector. He was charged by the grown-ups to look out for me, a duty he faithfully performed for the whole six months of my stay. He taught me how to make kites from palm leaves, how to catch lizards, which fruit to pick, and how to climb a coconut tree. He taught me all the Jamaican swearwords I know, and their meanings. There is a theme running through Jamaican swearwords to do with clothes, clothes intended to be used in regards to a variety of different body parts – clothes for bottoms, for example. In fact, bottoms themselves feature heavily in the armoury of insults. Robert, with his sidekick Pepito creasing up next to him, got me to say each swearword one-by-one, over and over again, before he divulged their true meanings to me, after which I was very careful never to use them in adult company.

It was Robert, backed up by creepy stories told by Eli, who also informed me about all the different types of Jamaican ghosts, and what to do if I caught sight of one. If I saw a common or garden duppy, I should tie my big toes together which would stop the ghoul in its tracks as all dead men were buried with their toes tied together. If I heard the scream of the fiery Rolling Calf I should run and hide, as there was no known defence against its other-worldly fury. If I saw the Obeah man on the beach I should run back home before he sacrificed me on the white sand. Where Robert started my health and safety education, Eli completed it. Eli's warnings even went beyond the supernatural into advice on how to avoid real-world dangers.

'If you swim out too far, unuh say hello to Mr Shark fi me.'

'If you see Mr Baraccuda, an im dart back like a snake, you betta swim fi your life cagh im wan' unuh fingers and toes fi im breakfast.'

'Gwan an play wi di vultures an dem will carry you off an feed you to dem chick dem.'

I never saw a Jamaican ghost, although everyone managed to convince me one night that a Rolling Calf had come by earlier calling for me by name, telling everyone he would be back later to find me. It was Robert's brainchild, who finished the prank off nicely by wailing his way into Granny's yard just after dusk, trailing a string of cans noisily behind him as I hid behind the tarpaulin, nearly dying of fright.

I only ever spotted one shark, rolling in the surf further down the beach where the seabed drops suddenly at high tide. I was relieved to be safely on the sand as I caught a glimpse of the shark, twice the size of me, pass by inside the rolling barrel. As for Mr Baraccuda, I never encountered him and lost no digits to his razor-sharp teeth. Vultures were my enemies whom I regularly chased with Kung Fu kicks and brandished sticks. They were so ugly and were more chicken than vulture. I had no encounters with the Obeah man so managed to keep my blood safe inside my veins. The threatening idea of him ready to end my life to please his gods kept me from straying too far down the beach on my own.

When there was a football match on, Robert would take me down into the bars the day before to collect empty pop cans. He taught me how to cut the metal and bend it into shape to form shrill, ear-piercing whistles, which we then sold for ten cents each for people to blow when their team scored a goal. The only time me and Robert ever fell out was when we disagreed on what to do with the proceeds of the whistle sale. Robert wanted to save the money we had made, to let it accumulate, or maybe to reinvest it into materials from which we could make better quality merchandise to sell for a bigger amount of profit. Robert had an acute business sense which I lacked. When we had made some change, I wanted to buy Jamaican patties, Bulla cake, and slices of Edam cheese. In the end we split all of our jointly and hard-earned dollars fifty-fifty, much to Robert's frustration. I stropped off to the shop and bought my food, which I came back to Robert with straightaway so that I could share it with him, just to prove that I wasn't a selfish English bwoy. He accepted my peace offering and we made some more whistles together. Robert also taught me how to string my plastic bottle seals into a long band, which in turn furnished the catapults we had whittled from sticks.

Robert and I became even closer when I got my own nickname, through a misadventure with the most royal of foodstuffs. I could write a whole chapter on delicious Jamaican foods, and maybe I will in another book someday. But best of all Jamaican foods, in my humble opinion, is the golden beef patty. The meat is tender and succulent, laced with scotch-bonnet pepper which burns the lips deliciously. Its turmeric laden pastry is crisp around the edges and soft in the middle. It is a thing of beauty and splendour, having the most exquisite flavour and texture. One single patty was somehow never enough, for me at least. This greed proved to be my downfall.

Mum bought me and her a patty each. I ate mine and enjoyed it very much. Mum decided that she would save hers for later, thinking that she would much prefer it after returning from the bars. She must have spotted an opportunistic glint in my eye as she left.

'I am leaving my patty to cool,' she said. 'I'll have it later. Do not eat it. I mean it. Just don't.'

'I won't. I'll look after it to make sure no-one else eats it.'

'It doesn't need you to look after it. Just keep out of my room and don't even touch it.'

'Okay Mum.'

Off Mum went, leaving me, and the patty. I could smell its succulent aroma through the closed bedroom door. Eventually I decided to skirt around the edge of temptation by stepping inside the room, hunting for the tasty pastry. It was not on the bed and nowhere to be seen on the dresser. Eventually I located it, hanging from a hook on the inside of the bedroom door in a brown paper bag. The bag was already greasy and see-through at the bottom corner, revealing a tantalising sight of the golden turmeric crust, bulging with peppery meat. I took it down gently, ever so gently, and held it under my nose so as to suck in the aroma, breathing deeply through my nostrils. Eventually I pulled it out of the bag, knowing I had lost the will to resist. I took a small nibble at the edge of the yellow crust, and then a bite, and then another bite, sinking my teeth into the soft middle-most parts. Before too long, all that remained was the back crust quivering between my fingers. This I also wanted to eat, but instead I mustered all of my strength and held back because this crust, this remnant, was now a crucial element sorely needed for my desperate recovery plan to work. I ripped the bottom of the paper bag, then placed it back on the hook on the back of the bedroom door. I crumbled off some crumbs from the crust onto the floor at the foot of the door below the hook and placed the crust strategically underneath the ripped paper bag. I then carefully made my exit, shedding a few more crumbs in a trail along the hallway as I slunk away.

Later, Mum returned, having enjoyed an evening of drinking white rum and coke and watching men play dominoes. She made straight for her bedroom, seeking that morsel which she had told me to leave. I had to make my play before she realised for herself that something was amiss.

'Mum, I heard something.'

'Eh, what? What do you mean?'

'I heard something fall onto the floor in your room.' I could hear my own voice, cracked and feeble, lacking any trace of conviction.

'What fell on the floor?'

'Your patty, I heard it fall....'

'What?' Mum entered her room with me trailing nervously behind. There were ants on the floor, attacking the meagre crust.

'I heard it fall Mum.'

Mum lifted the torn bag from the hook and sat on the bed, waiting patiently for the rest of my fabrication.

'I didn't do anything at first but then I went to the toilet and saw a big ant with a piece of patty in its pincers and there was a line of crumbs so I opened the door and saw your patty on the floor well some of it and the ants were all over it and...'

Mum looked at me with steely green eyes, like a hungry cat about to pounce. Then her face softened. She laughed and laughed, with an almost silent wheeze. She kept laughing, waving her hand in the air, then holding her side.

'Big ants.... big ants... Ah Dougie. Big ants...'

I was suddenly thankful for the calming effects of strong white rum.

'The steam from the patty must have made the paper bag soggy and the patty must have just slipped out because of its weight and the ants would have smelt it and there was a line of ants in the hall carrying crumbs so I....'

Even I did not believe my story as my words trailed off in the face of Mum's persistent and now uncontrollable laughter.

After my confession, eased as it was by Mum's good humour, word soon got out around Granny's yard, and further afield that Mary's boy had eaten Mary's patty and blamed it on the ants. My punishment for this food theft was being branded with the fitting name, first uttered by the victim of the crime: Big Ants.

Robert, AKA Big Rat, was perhaps the most amused by my new alias.

'Big Ants. Woiiiii! Big Ants. Eh, Big Ants, you like a bit a Patty een?'

'Eh, Big Ants. You wan mi fi fetch you another pattie now?'

'But wait. So you hear de pattie drop 'pon de floor. Awo. Den you see de ants a carry de crumbs down de corridor. Awo. Den you see a giant ant a tek de patty and eat de whole ting. Awo. It mus a been a Big Ant!'

And on, and on, and on. But it brought me and Robert even closer together and we became as thick as thieves. My friendship with Big Rat was one of the surprising things that happened to me in Jamaica. I appreciated his care, protection and patience beyond measure.

Robert told me repeatedly not to fight in the stone wars during lunchtimes at school. He was concerned that I would be injured, or worse. He told me stories of boys getting killed by rock-blows to the head, or having their eyes gouged out by the enemy. But I ignored him. Lunchtime was the most exciting part of my school day by far.

We poured out of the gate as soon as the bell rang, purchasing sticky coconut brittle and ice pops from the stalls outside. The Yallahs School Army then entered the arena of battle, the field outside the school gates, and collected their missiles. I was a soldier in the YSA, skilled in Kung Fu and deadly in the art of slingshot. My skin colour was completely irrelevant; I was an equal with my companions. I took the same risks, felt the same surge of adrenaline when the enemy chased us, jumped as high as anyone in elation when the enemy retreated into the trees.

There were many legends about the enemy, of what they were capable of – their brutality, and bad treatment of anyone they managed to capture. The 'enemy' were the children from the village in the trees, the nameless ones who did not go to school. Their village could be glimpsed amidst the trees at the far side of the field. Every lunch time they emerged as we collected stones to sling and sticks to fight with. As we advanced against our enemy, slings would whir around letting stones sail into the air. The scorching sun was high in the cloudless sky as sweat trickled down my back. The Village Army charged, and we retreated, and then rallied, as stones zipped past overhead, or fell disappointingly short. In all the days of lunchtime war, I never witnessed a single injury on either side. Fear of capture kept the two sides at a healthy distance from each other, rendering our ammunition mostly ineffective. Sometimes, towards the end of the lunchtime break, when everyone was tired and hot, we would be close enough to the other side to see their smiling faces as they waved us back into the safety of the school gates.

We saw them once on the way home from school, standing on a small bridge waving to us.

Robert went over to them alone and talked with them. Robert knew absolutely everyone and was on good terms with most. As we waved goodbye to them that day, I got my clearest ever sight of their smiling faces – just boys and girls, like us, with nothing better to do at lunchtime. My regret is that I did not speak to them face-to-face, or visit their village hidden in the trees. It chills me now to think that we used to search for broken plastic spectacle frames with metal spikes protruding, which bizarrely were scattered across the field, to arm ourselves in case of capture. Tooled up at age nine, I dread to imagine what may have occurred had the two opposing sides ever made contact in the middle of the dry, cowpat-strewn field.

The way home from school, escorted by Robert, often held adventure of some sort. There was the day we walked through an open funeral, with loud organ music playing as distraught relatives wailed as they passed by the open coffin. It was the first time I had ever seen a dead person. Then there was the slaughter of the cow. Tied to a tree, its throat was slit releasing a crimson spray from its neck as it weakened and finally fell to its knees in the searing heat. The hot walk home, over the dry riverbed and on through Yallahs Bay, would always be rewarded with a dip in the sea before we made our way back up the hill to Granny's yard, where rice and peas and chicken and spice would be cooking away in Granny's hut.

I knew that living in Jamaica for six months would

change me, but the way it changed me was surprising. It was another stage in my journey from little boy to young man. I had learned the art of lunchtime war and the deadly art of Jamaican Kung Fu. They called me Big Ants, assassin of the night. Nothing encrusted in golden turmeric pastry was ever safe again.

## 20

# MANY RIVERS TO CROSS

'Too many rivers to cross' by Jimmy Cliff was Mum's favourite song in 1980. I watched her as she sang it, wondering what she was thinking as she swayed with her swollen belly in Eli's arms on the porch of Granny's house. I felt her emotion and without comprehension enjoyed it as the organ music and the silky smooth vocals of Jimmy Cliff washed over me. Mum's adventure in Jamaica was peppered with love, loss and longing, all pickled in Uncle Wray's over-proof white rum.

As I walked on the bridge over the stony dry riverbed on the way to and from school, I often wondered why the riverbed was so wide, yet so dry. The day that it rained, I found my answer. Granny had been warning us all for days that the rain was coming. Then one morning she ran out of the house saying "Look now! De rain it a come." I looked to where Granny was pointing. I saw a long ridge of cloud in the distance. Then, as it got nearer, I saw a curtain of rain advancing over the ground faster than I could run. It was one of the strangest sights I have ever seen. It was dry and sunny where we were, but over there it was pouring down with heavy rain behind the wet curtain. Mum came out into the yard holding her bump and stood beside me.'You just wait for this Dougie. Don't run inside, just stand in it. You'll see.'

The wet curtain finally reached the yard and washed over us. It was warm – bathwater warm, at first, at least. Children danced with their mouths wide open as Mum and I stood in the warm shower together, palms and smiling faces upturned.

Then it rained and rained all day and all night. The clouds became thicker and darker, the rain became heavier and colder, and the thunder and lightning started as Granny pulled the tarpaulin around the veranda. The next morning it was still pouring. The path down to Yallahs Bay had become a fast-flowing stream, and on the way to school I saw my one and only Jamaican river in full flow. What had been a dry, rocky channel was now a mighty river in full flow, almost bursting its banks.

The rain lasted for days and days, turning the normally dry heat into an overbearing tropical humidity, and the nights into cold, thundery storms. The rain was also accompanied by toads, thousands upon thousands of them, everywhere. They would hop through the yard and get squashed on the roads by cars and lorries. I must have stepped on at least fifty of them by accident. They were countless and made a huge noise.

The day the rain stopped, I watched the trailing curtain disappear out of sight, like the coming of it days before, only in reverse. When it had passed, it only took a few hours for the land to return to its formerly parched state, although the plants were all greener, and grass and wild flowers had grown along the path where before it had been only dust. The flow of the river eventually slowed, then stopped, exposing the dry riverbed once again.

Mum had many rivers to cross, the saddest of which was the loss of her first daughter. She was taken to the hospital by Eli in haste after some bleeding and I was left with Granny. When Eli returned in the evening, grief-stricken at the loss of his daughter, I cried and cried. It was such a sad time in which everyone we knew shed tears on Mary and Eli's behalf. The baby girl had been overdue but had died during labour with the umbilical cord wrapped around her neck. When Mum returned from the hospital days later, she was angry. She said that the hospital did not have the right equipment to save the baby. Mum said that her daughter would have survived if she had been born in England.

After this tragedy, Mum and Eli argued a lot more behind their closed bedroom door. Eli would emerge from the bedroom, visibly dejected, leaving Mum to cry or shout or stew in silence. When Mum emerged, she was a woman on a mission.

'Dougie, we're going to the market to sell some of our clothes.'

She stuffed all her maternity clothes into a case, and off we went on the Island Bus to Morrant Bay to make some dollars. We hung all the brightly coloured dresses and tops on the wire fence at the edge of the market and sat in the sun as Mum's maternal wardrobe was eagerly snapped away item by item. We ended that day talking to an English lady who had a house by the beach. She invited us back for tea before we took the hair-raising Island Bus journey back to Yallahs through the steep, wooded hills.

It was election time in Jamaica and the build-up to election day was a bloody affair. People were being shot because of their politics. The shopkeeper down in Yallahs was murdered. A man was shot standing right next to my Mum whilst she was drinking in a bar. Mum said she saw the car stop outside. The window wound down, the gun pointing at the man next to her, then the bang, followed by the car pulling away as the man next to her collapsed onto the floor. There were posters everywhere. 'Vote Edward Seaga,' or 'Michael Manley for President.' Edward Seaga became the fifth Jamaican President in 1980, beating Michael Manley after an election which saw over 800 people murdered purely over politics.

Granny and Eli seemed largely unconcerned by politics though. Granny was far too busy cooking and cleaning and running the household in the absence of Grandpa Tailor, who had died many years earlier. I was exploring at the back of Granny's garden once and found myself standing on his white tomb. First there was a tickle on the leg, and then a sharp pain, then another sharp pain. I looked down at my bare legs, and saw the hugest, reddest ants I have ever seen. I could see their jaws at the front of their massive heads. I could see them spraying my legs and making them sting. I padded my feet and brushed them off but more and more came scurrying out of nowhere to eat me alive. Eventually I had the sense to get off the stone and run away, much to the amusement of all who saw the sore stings on the backs of my legs.

Eli was very busy building an extension on the back of Granny's house which I helped him with when I could, carrying things or mixing cement. He was also quite busy doing business with the mango canning factory, as well as the tobacco-growing farmer. He and Mum would disappear for days at a time to the factory or the fields. They were arranging to buy a large crop of tobacco, and for it to be canned in mango tins, so that they could transport it back to England. I didn't really pay much attention to the matter until Eli and Mum came back with a large bag full of 'tobacco'. The green leaves were laid out on the white stones under the pomegranate tree in Granny's yard to dry in the sun. When I saw the feathery five-pointed leaves, and smelt their pungent aroma, I knew they were 'weed' leaves, not tobacco. On the way back to England, Mum and I flew on a separate plane to Eli. At the airport in London, a man with a clipboard followed my Mum through the airport all the way to the exit doors, asking lots of questions about our holiday, about Eli, and about the trolley which Mum was pulling behind her. It was heavily laden with mango tins.

Whilst I was in Jamaica, my relationship with Eli flourished. He warmed to me and took me under his wing as much as he could. It was an amazing feeling for me to be welcomed into his mother's home, to become part of his wider family. There was one day that he took Mum and me on a long walk along the coast to see one of his friends. I walked between Eli and Mum along the white beaches, through the shaded coconut plantation, he in his white brimmed hat, and Mum in her shades and sarong. Eli allowed me to carry his machete and taught me how to split the husk of a fresh coconut, to chop off the top to get to the refreshing, clear milk inside. There is nothing like fresh coconut milk, followed by scoops of jelly coconut flesh. Eli's friend caught us a lobster which Eli let me try when we returned to Granny's house.

Eli became more than willing to interact with me. He provided me with a good example of what a father should be, supplying a steady calmness which provided good soil for mine and Mum's relationship to grow. He also provided discipline on the odd occasion when the need arose.

Food was delicious in Jamaica but it was not always plentiful. I ate most things but could not muster the inner strength needed to make myself eat chicken-foot soup. I felt that it was necessary at times to supplement my diet with sweet, raw energy – brown sugar. Granny kept the brown sugar in a pot in the cabinet in the dining room. I knew exactly where it was. I tried a few daylight raids but these were too risky and had to be too hasty to gain any real benefit. So I decided to try out a night time raid. The first few times were successful, not taking too much, and not spilling any. Then one night I became a little too greedy and careless. I had taken enough for Granny to be sure some was indeed missing and I had spilt some of the brown granules onto the dining room table. They were on to the thief in the night, although they could not yet prove it was me. So foolishly, I did it again.

It was dark and everyone except me was fast asleep. I crept through the darkness, hoping I would not accidentally step onto a scorpion or a spider. I opened the cabinet door fast, so as not to allow it to squeak an alarm, and pulled out the sugar. Placing it gently on the table, I pulled out the cork stopper and plunged my hand into the wide rimmed glass jar. Back went my head as my fingers, loaded with cane sugar, plunged into my open mouth. Then the door flew open and the lights came on. I jumped, spilling sugar onto the floor. Eli entered the room with a wry smile on his face and a slipper in his hand.

'Caught you at it child. You too dyam noisy. If you gonna steal sugar you should a been quiet about it, and neva leave such a mess.'

I watched him as I trailed around the table, keeping it as safety between him and me. I was embarrassed and totally rumbled.

'Get back in a ya bed byow. I'll deal with you in de marnin.'

I had witnessed discipline Jamaican style and did not want any to come my way. A young girl had been 'switched' in the yard by her mother, who held onto her wrist as the pair turned in circle after circle, the stick thrashing the girl's bottom as she ran in a futile attempt to avoid the blows. There was usually a build-up. Word quite often got around that someone had committed a wrong and were headed towards a beating. There was usually a gap between the misbehaviour and the punishment. The punishment was usually planned, and measured, and unemotional, at least for the administrator of justice.

My punishment was no different. Eli kept his beady eye on me all through the breakfast of fried dumplings and ackee and saltfish, and into the morning. I kept my distance, watching his every move in the hope that I would detect his attempt to grab me. I need not have worried so much since he gave me ample warning of what was to come. He turned towards me and slid off his belt. He bent his belt in two, taking a firm grip, and then advanced towards me. I ran and darted, pumped with adrenaline. Everyone watched me, some with half-hidden smiles, as the drama played out. The tension had mounted all morning in Granny's yard because everyone knew what was coming. All of my Kung Fu training became suddenly useless in this real-life battle of wits.

Eventually, I played my hand by jumping up into the tree. Eli knew this would be my end. There was only one branch low enough to reach and shin across, along which Eli followed me. I sat straddled on the end of it looking down and trying to calculate how much the drop would hurt my feet. Eli shimmied closer and closer, belt in hand. When he was close enough to take a swing, I cocked my leg over and hung by my hands. I looked down as Eli drew his hand back with a glint in his eye. Thwack. The distance was too great to drop. Thwack. The stones below were too bumpy to land safely on, even with sandled feet. Thwack. The blows were not as hard, or as painful, as I feared they might be, but just real enough to be uncomfortable. Eventually, I braced myself and let go. I landed on my feet but fell backwards onto my bottom in the dry white dust of the yard. Everyone just creased up. My bottom hurt a bit, just a little bit, but that was mostly from the fall. I laughed. Eli laughed as he looked down at me from the tree. I had been disciplined, with mercy, Jamaican style. And I never, ever stole the cane sugar again.

The saddest part of my relationship with Eli for me was when he didn't take me with him into the mountains. His father, Grandpa Tailor, had a plot in the mountains behind Yallahs where fruit and vegetables of all kinds grew – yams, plantain, breadfruit, sweet potatoes, papaya, mangoes, lemons, limes and many other important foodstuffs. As he prepared his expedition, I begged him for days to take me with him but he refused. I held onto the hope that he would change his mind, right up to the moment he walked out of Granny's yard with all the other boys, including Robert and Peppito, but not me.

'Me nah g'wan tek you pitney. We camping out with spiders and snakes. Is not safe fi unnu.'

'But you're taking all the others.'

'Them is used to it. You is not. You g'wan stay with unuh mamma.'

He led the donkey and the boys away and up Newlands Road into the mountains, leaving me with the women and girls. If only he had trusted me. If only he had believed in me, that I could cope and work. When they had gone, I took myself off alone into the forest at the top of Newlands Road, catapult in hand, hunting for birds. When Eli and the boys returned two days later, with a donkey laden with fruit and vegetables, Eli gave me a big slice of paw-paw, my absolute favourite fruit.

When I had first arrived in Jamaica, I was a fragile white bwoy, coming straight from dar England. The mosquitoes loved my sweet blood and massacred my legs. I had to put yellow ointment on the sores and endure the nickname 'fossy-foot' for a time. I had become delirious with fever after a bout of weapons-grade diarrhoea on the way back up the track to Granny's yard. Khaki shorts. Not good. I then spent days sleeping in a sweat, or staggering around the house in half a dream. I adapted and survived. Before I left Jamaica, no mosquito could touch me. My ears were fine-tuned to their high-pitched whine, and any attempt to pierce my skin was met with a swift slap, leading to death by splat. I could eat all the food, drink all the water, pluck a chicken, shell the peas, wash my own clothes. I could speak fluent patois at breakneck speed, eat bird-peppers, and devour as much Jamaican food as anyone would pass my way. At nine years of age I had become, culturally at least, part-Jamaican. Mum had stayed very English indeed and it was the one time in my life that I had successfully managed to out-Jamaica her.

One of the last things I did in Jamaica was go down to the beach with Eli and Robert early in the morning to watch the sun rise from the edge of the sea. I could hear Luke Skywalker's theme tune playing in my head as the waves washed onto the shore. Then we followed a procession of people in robes along the beach, who were singing hymns and dancing in the early morning light. They stopped, baptised some of their number in the sea, then danced and sang all the way back up to the church at the end of Granny's yard.

Our final Jamaican meal was bad news for Granny's goat. Apart from Jamaican brown chicken and rice and peas, curried goat is my second favourite Jamaican dish and I appreciate the sacrifice that grumpy goat, who would never allow me to milk it, made. I was warned that it would be hot, which it was, but I loved it all the same. My love for Jamaican food has endured to this day; cooked on occasion in my own home, my favourite meal out with my family or friends has to be a trip to Turtle Bay for brown chicken and a shot of Uncle Wrays.

It was a wrench for me to leave Jamaica. Mum, mourning as she was for her first daughter, had a good support network in Eli and his family. She was still mother to me, and to all the other children in Granny's yard, and was happy most of the time. I was enjoying life – the food, Friday night Kung Fu cinema, the beach, friendship with Robert. My very last night in Jamaica was spent gambling under the streetlight on Newlands Road with the older kids and Robert, which I was not usually allowed to do. I was desperately trying to lose all of Mum's loose change before we left. Bats and bugs whirred past in the lamplight as we bent low and rolled cent coins along the road towards the wall.

When all of our cases were packed into the boot of the white taxi early in the morning, we all said our goodbyes. I promised to write to Robert and gave all of my toys away, including my collection of Star Wars figurines. My panda bear went to a little girl who hugged it and stood smiling at me. Mum hugged all of the children, giving special attention to Peppito, who had become her favourite. Eli and Granny cried and embraced and Granny gave Mum, then me, a big hug too.

'Tek care of each other now. Visit again when you can. You are always welcome here.'

A while later, as we stepped out of the sliding airport doors into the cold rain of England, my Jamaican dreams began to fade.

I had traversed from Derby, then to Jamaica, and then to London.

London City was lying in wait for us, ready to cage us up inside a council flat.

This would be where our ride together really began to get darker.

'Hold on tight.'

# 21

# LONDON'S DARK CLOUD

My dressing gown was black, with one golden dragon flashing fire from its eyes. My pose in the long mirror was tiger-claw, sideways on with one leg up ready to kick. Then I spread my arms wide as I stooped low into preying-mantis fist, fingers stiff, poised to strike. I was a Jamaican boy in London, ready to fight all challengers.

Eli looked at me from his chair, clutching his stomach in pain because of his ulcer. 'No bother try unuh kung-fu magic 'pon pitney-dem in a your school Dominic, you hear me? You start dancin' around like a idiot, dem gonna box you fi sure.'

I regarded him with steel in my eyes, trying not to betray my true feeling of thankfulness that he cared what happened to me in the strange, English school. But I did not stop my daily routine. Did he not know that I was now a master of all styles of Sholin Kung-Fu? Besides, I may yet have need to fight at school.

When the London boys, some of whom were of Afro-Caribbean heritage first heard my patois, they had questions.

'Nah man, he's taking the mick. Talk normal. You're not even black.'

'Me ciaaant help it, is jus de way mi-a talk. Dem talk like dis in Jamaica.'

'Naaaah man, you're just being extra innit. You better stop it man or you'll get your ed kicked in.'

Things became easier when they realised that I wasn't faking it. Indignation was replaced by curiosity and threats to kill subsided. I quickly became good friends with the cool bunch due to my interesting six month holiday and my fluency in patois. My one and only regret about having lived in Jamaica was that the patois almost totally erased my Derbyshire accent. In time, patios drifted into abrupt South London leaving only one discernibly 'Northern' trait. If I said bus, or duck, or similar words, the 'u' would hardly ever turn into an 'a', like it did for my new friends. But just as I had prized my Derbyshire-ness, so now I realised that I also prized my Jamaican-ness. I did not want my patois to fade. I did not want to become English again.

Life in Mrs Bunyan's class at Springfield Junior School took some getting used to. It was so noisy, not like Jamaica where we had studied in complete silence. It felt like chaos at first as I sat at my desk wondering when someone was going to get the cane out. That never happened. I felt let down on the one and only time I had ever been sent to the headmaster's office for misbehaving. Mr Daley peered over his glasses at me, frowning with his bushy eyebrows.

'Come here boy and put your hand out.'

He produced a soft blue slipper from behind his

back. Slop. That was it.

'I don't want to see you in here again.' He didn't, not for being naughty anyway.

The school had a particular feeling about it. It was earmarked for closure, with our year due to be the last intake. When we all left at the end of year six, Springfield Primary School would be no more.

The quietest time at school was the end of the day when we had story time. Mrs Bunyan would read a chapter at a time to the whole class. As I sat listening I was transported away through deep fur-lined wardrobes to snow-covered woods to meet fauns and talking lions. I was swept away under sea and over stone as the menacing darkness rose, casting shadows across grey Welsh mountains and a silver tree on the Malvern Hills. There were ancient knights awakened from tombs hidden deep inside magic mounds as children fought monsters and dark enemies, in alliance with wizards and kings. Mrs Bunyan led me into worlds of fantasy and magic with her silken voice, always pausing for effect at the right moments.

I took those books home with me and read, and read, and read. The child-heroes in those books were powerful and protected, always dancing on the edge of danger and ruin. Their worlds gave me somewhere to escape to when I needed 'out' of real life, which for me had taken a dark turn.

*

On the 6th August 1981, five months after returning to England, the sky turned unnaturally dark in South London at mid-afternoon. As I emerged from the community hall, where I had just watched the film Battle Beyond the Stars, it felt like I was stepping into another science fiction movie. People were out on the streets, looking up at the dark sky, asking if it was an eclipse. As the street lamps flickered on, it felt like night had fallen on Hemans Estate on the Wandsworth Road. No-one could see even the shadow of a sun. Thick black clouds rolled silently overhead until the lightning began, with peals of distant thunder breaking the eerie silence. Flash, rumble. Flash, flash, rumble, rumble, rumble. It felt like the end of the world.

The sun had been blotted out but not by the moon. It was the eight mile high cumulonimbus storm cloud – which had just discharged most of its hail and rain over Surrey – that was blotting out the sun's light over South-West London. It had travelled all the way from the continent, bringing its last oppressive hours to bear upon Hemans Estate. It was almost frightening. The consensus among the sky-watchers was that there was no eclipse, and no-one on Hemans Estate knew anything about super-sized European storm clouds on that day.

An absence of light began to roll over my home life as well, causing storms at times. Mum's anger flashed like lightning, followed by rumbling peals of clumsy discipline administered alone and in the heat of the moment. When we arrived in London, we had stayed with Eli's relatives in Brixton. Then Eli had opened up a squat for us on Hemans Estate in a block which was due for demolition. He had been present at first, often taking me to work with him where I would help mask out car windows before he would spray the doors with paint. He would let me have some of his Irish Moss drink with seaweed, condensed milk and vanilla, as well as a bottle of Supermalt, all to myself. He and Mum started to argue pretty much as soon as we began living on the estate. Mum had not long ago lost her first daughter in a foreign country and now she was carrying her third child, my eldest sister. It was a time of uncertainty and instability for her. The arguments got worse and worse, with shouting and screaming, banging and throwing, followed by squally showers. Eli spent less and less time with us in the flat, leaving Mum largely alone in a lonely, strange place with a ten year-old boy who she barely knew.

It was mostly laziness, or badly done chores, that got me into trouble with Mum. I could never tell exactly when the weather would turn at home but sometimes I could feel the atmosphere changing. Once the sky darkened and the curtain of cold rain descended, there was no going back.

'I thought I told you to sweep the hall. Look, there's still dirt on the floor. You wouldn't have got away with this at Granny's house.'

'Mum, I have done it. I did, honest.'

'You liar. You haven't even moved the brush.'

'I have. I put it back Mum...'

'No you didn't. I hate it when you tell me lies.'

'But Mum...'

'Right. Come here. I'll teach you to tell me lies.'

At first it was her slipper, then her leather belt, then, the buckle at the end of her leather belt. Mum would chase me around the small, dark flat. When she finally had a firm grip of my arm, we would dance together in a circle as Mum's discipline rained down upon my legs, buttocks and back.

Some days were quiet, some were not. When Eli was in, he and Mum argued and I was forgotten. When Eli was away, I just wanted him back. I would come home from school, watch Danger Mouse, eat tea, and do the washing up. Then we would dance.

'You call this washing up? How many times have I told you to use the scratchy green bit of the sponge to do the cutlery? How many times?'

'I did Mum. I did...'

'Look at this. And this. Don't bother telling me you have when you haven't.'

'I thought I had Mum...'

'Well you know what thought did don't you. I'll teach you to do sloppy washing up. Come here...'

Sometimes I could see why Mum was angry but sometimes I really couldn't. When I was at home I focused my attention on my jobs, especially the washing up. The water had to be hot. You always washed the glasses first in hot, but not very hot, water, otherwise they would crack. Then you would put in more hot water to do the plates and mugs whilst the cutlery soaked at the bottom. My fingertips would inspect the surface of each plate, as missed dried-on food would always be spotted. You used the brillo pad for the steel pans, but never the non-stick pans. You used the green pad of the sponge on the black Dutchie pot, so that you got all the food off but left the blackness on the surface. You never used the abrasive top. Each piece of cutlery needed to be washed individually, starting with the eating end and always moving down to cover the handle between tightly squeezed fingers. The most important parts of the cutlery to watch were between the prongs of the forks and the tea-stains on the teaspoons. Then last you would rinse the pans and then drain the dirty water. Then you would fill the sink again and rewash the pans to make sure no grease remained. When all was clean you would pass each item under the running cold tap to rinse the soap off. You did this carefully as Mum could tell when she used a plate, or a mug, if it still had soap on it. Sometimes the consequence would be a gentle reminder, sometimes focused rage.

No matter how hard I tried to clean properly, be on time, say the right things, not say the wrong things, there was eventually a slipup on my part, or an unfavourable decision on Mum's. Once, after Mum had punished me, she turned to me with a relieved expression on her face.

'There, that's better isn't it? At least we've cleared the air between us.'

But my air was still filled with dark clouds.

When I was beaten by the buckle of the belt, it left bruises and red, raised welts on my lower back and buttocks. It was sore to sit down or to lie on my back. Because it was a P.E. day at school, I was not allowed to take my kit in.

'You don't need to do P.E. every flipping time they tell you to. Just say you forgot your kit. And don't take your jumper off.'

When it came to P.E. time, I made my excuses.

'I forgot my kit sir.'

'Not to worry, just make sure you bring it next time OK?'

Off I slunk towards the gym benches at the side of the hall, that is until the P.E. teacher stopped me in my tracks.

'You can still join in young man, even without your kit. Just take your jumper off.'

*Just take your jumper off. Just don't take your jumper off.*

'I'm fine sir, I don't want to take my...'

'You can't climb ropes in that big sweaty thing. Take it off.'

Off came the jumper. It was longer than my school shirt and looser. It didn't ride up so much when I lifted my arms. I knew what was coming. If you had asked me at that moment after I had carefully taken the jumper off what was coming next, I could have told you.

It was my turn to climb the rope. I approached the thick rope, dangling from the track on the high ceiling. With my arms raised half-height I made a feeble start. It was difficult clambering up the rope without allowing my arms to stretch out fully. As I inched higher and higher my elbows were torn away from my ribs, moving past my shoulders, then my ears as I pulled myself up. I hung at the top, hands high above my head with arms outstretched, feeling air on my lower back. I wondered if anyone could see the red welts from the hall floor below.

I stood at the bottom of the rope with the teacher. He looked at me and asked the question I knew was coming. It was like being in the ancient garden again; everything was darkly familiar.

'How did you get those marks Dominic?'

'I fell over and banged myself on the edge of my metal bed.'

'On your bed?'

'Yes.'

I was called into Mr Daley's office after the P.E. session. He spoke slowly and kindly. I had never heard him use this tone before.

'Now tell me what has happened at home Dominic. How did you get those red marks all over your back?'

'I fell off my bed, sir, and banged my back on the edge of it.'

'Hmm, fell off your bed. Do you mind if I have a look at the marks Dominic?'

'No, sir.'

I stood up and un-tucked my shirt, lifting it up to my midriff. Tears brimmed in my eyes as anger bubbled inside me. This was all the P.E. teacher's fault for making me take my jumper off in the first place anyway.

'Sit down, sit down. So, Dominic, I'm quite concerned about those marks on your back so I am going to phone your mother and ask her to come in and speak to me. Is she at home today?'

'No, she's out shopping today. She won't be back until later.'

'Well, I'll try her all the same. Was your mother there when you fell off the bed?'

'Erm, yes, she was.'

'So she will give the same explanation?'

'Yes, I think so Sir. I think she saw me fall off my bed anyway.'

When you tell a lie to a person who is being kind to you, it magnifies the guilt about ten times. It also raises the stakes. Every time you confirm the lie, every time you back up what you have already said happened – which of course did not happen – you put extra emotional chips on the table. Raise me two. Ten. A hundred. Will Mum say the same thing? Will this gamble pay off? If only I could get to speak to Mum before Mr Daley does. The other worry was that I had disobeyed Mum's direct instruction not to take my jumper off. I knew that I would also have to answer for that.

Later on I was called back into Mr Daley's office, where he and Mum sat waiting for me. Mum had been crying.

'I just don't know what to do with him Mr Daley. I try, I try so hard...' Mum started to cry again and reached out to me. As I stood, she pulled me towards her and hugged me.

'I try so hard with him but I just don't know what to do sometimes. I just lost my temper with him. I didn't mean to hurt him... I didn't mean to...'

'Well Miss White, it's important that we deal properly with these sorts of things. You can't beat your son like this, no matter what he has done.'

'I need help though Mr Daley. You don't see what he's like at home. He needs discipline. I can't just let him do what he wants. He's got to pull his weight.'

'Hmm, yes, well Miss White, I agree that you do need some help. What I am going to do is call the Education Welfare Department to see if they can provide some assistance.'

'What's that, social services? No I don't want to see any more of them. They're useless. They never help. I don't want you to involve them, thank you very much.'

'Well, I will be making a referral...'

'A referral. What?' Mum lost some of her composure and stood up. 'I'll tell you what, you haven't got a clue how he behaves have you? He's all sweetness and light when he's at school but he's not the same when he's at home. You only see one side of him. He swears at me. You should be helping him more when he's at school. You should be taking the time to ask him what he does at home.'

'Miss White, please sit down and...'

Mum left quickly, shooting me a glance and leaving me in the chair in front of Mr Daley. From that moment I wanted that school day to last forever. When Mrs Bunyan started to read, I never wanted her to stop.

An idea of Jamaican discipline had travelled over the Atlantic Ocean, on a Boeing 747, in the mind of Mary of Derby who herself was a survivor – one to whom life had given no favours. The essence of this Jamaican discipline had become corrupted like a contaminated seed. Gone were the roots of forethought, composure, intention. It had become an emotional affair, impulsive and mostly irrational. Gone was the refining effect of public humiliation and social shame. We danced in private where no-one else could see and in spite of my extensive Kung Fu skills, I couldn't fight back.

The only place I could run to were the magic lands of the stories I was being told with their grey wolves on Welsh mountains and talking beavers in snow-covered lands. There was magic and adventure to be found in the shadow of Cader Idris, that ancient Welsh mountain, or in Narnia with the White Queen and her Turkish Delight. The real world was dark, as if a great eight mile-high cloud had blotted out the Sun. But there was always a brighter landscape to escape to, within the pages of Mrs Bunyan's enchanting books.

*

'Dominic was first referred to me in June 1982 whilst a pupil at Springfield Primary School and Miss

White sent a letter to the Headmaster complaining about Dominic's behaviour at home. Mr Daley the Headmaster at Springfield was concerned about this as he found Dominic a very pleasant pupil at the school and thought perhaps there was something wrong at home.'

(Mrs J C, Education Welfare Officer. 11th April 1985).

# 22

# BECOMING LIKE CALVIN

Mum was pregnant again and Eli was in the house less and less. When he was, there were arguments in which they swore at each other – Eli with his sing-song Jamaican poetry about cloths for various body parts, and Mum's proper English insults scooped out of the linguistic gutter. Things would smash and doors would slam. Mum burst into my bedroom in tears once whilst I was playing 'Prince Charming' by Adam and the Ants. The front door had just slammed loudly.

'I threw an iron at him... I think he's gone for good this time.'

'Was the iron hot, Mum?' I was worried about Eli.

'Yes... Yes it was. I was ironing with it. I think I've blown it...'

'Did it hit him, Mum?'

'Yes, he's bleeding...'

'Where is he bleeding, Mum? Where did the iron hit him?'

'On the head, on his head Dougie... I hope he's all right...'

Eli returned a couple of days later and Mum cooked a pan-full of homemade oxtail soup with boiled dumplings.

When Eli was away, out at work, or staying with relatives, Mum focussed her attention on me. We had been visited by a lady from the Education Welfare Department whom Mum had spoken to calmly with a tight-lipped smile. The school needed to help me with my behaviour at home, according to Mum. I can't remember what the lady said, but nothing changed.

'Look, there's still dust in the hall. You lied. You didn't even pick up the brush. Look, it's in exactly the same place as I left it. I can see it hasn't even been moved.'

'I did it, Mum. I did sweep the hall. You're always picking on me for things I haven't done...'

'Yeah, for things you haven't done. Anyway, I'm not picking on you. I'm disciplining you. I have to. If I don't do this, who else will? No-one at your school is man enough to sort you out and Eli won't help me. I'm all you've got. You haven't got a dad who will discipline you, so it's me I'm afraid.'

We danced in painful circles. It reminded me of ballet. I would be on my toes, hopping in a circle, one hand guarding my bottom and one hand held high in Mum's grasp. Mum would follow me around with the belt, lashing and lashing. The movement of the dance would render many thrashes ineffective but a few would be well-timed – suddenly a sharp pain on my ear, or shoulder, causing me to put my hand up, then the real strike, always lower, finding unprotected skin.

'Ow, Mum! I didn't do it.'

'Mum, I did do it.'

'Mum, I won't do it again.'

'Mum, I'll do it again.'

*Mum, why are you doing this? Where are you? Where have you gone? I can't make you happy with me, no matter what I do, no matter how hard I try. How can I make you happy with me? How can I bring you back? When I look into your eyes, I see hatred and loathing. Do you blame me for something? Do you think that it was my fault that you lost your baby? Was it my fault? I just want you to see me again.*

'You've got to earn my trust back. How can I trust you when you lie to me?'

*I don't lie to you Mum. I have nothing to lie about. I do my best. Washing up is hard sometimes. I know how to do it but I can't always get it right. Sometimes I miss things by accident, never on purpose. I never put a plate on the rack with dried food still on it and think, 'I wonder if Mum will spot that.' I just don't do that, Mum. When I'm sweeping the hall or the bathroom or my bedroom, I never leave dust or hair in the corner on purpose for you to find. I don't leave bits just to see what your reaction will be. I don't forget things on purpose, things that you told me to do. I just forget sometimes. I just genuinely forget.*

*Why does how you feel affect me so much? Can't you see Mum? It's not my behaviour that decides if I need discipline or not. It's how you feel inside. They say we take it out on those we love. Is this your way of loving me, Mum? Is this love that I'm feeling?*

That flat in Hemans House became a dark place. There was one evening when I had to go to bed early. It was dark and I felt strange. It was not a normal evening, or a normal bedtime, but I could not say exactly why. Mum was insistent that I had my bedroom light off but that night I was afraid of being in the dark. I lay in bed, having turned the light back on, waiting for Mum to notice. Then the door opened and the light went off. There were no other lights visible in the flat under the crack of my door. It was pitch black. I plucked up enough courage to jump out of my metal bed and made a dash to the light switch by the door. On it flickered as I ran back to my bed. Doors outside swished, feet padded and my door flew open again. Off went the light.

'Keep the light off. I won't tell you again.'

'But I'm scared Mum...'

'Of what? You mardy baby, there's nothing to be scared of. It's only the dark. Now keep it off.'

It felt like something else was in the room with me, something sinister. Just getting back out of bed took all my willpower. I ran to the switch with my eyes tight shut. When the light came on the uneasy feeling subsided, yet a trace of it lingered. There was an atmosphere in the flat that night which I can't explain. Perhaps there was something going on with me; an illness, or being half-awake or something like that. Or maybe it was something bad in the flat, something in my room.

The door swished, the feet padded, then nothing – some clunking, but no opening my bedroom door. Then all of a sudden, without the door opening, the light went out. I was instantly freaked, imagining that the presence in my room had flicked the switch. I jumped out of bed, disorientated, and somehow managed to find the light switch on the wall by the door. Flick. Flick. Flick. Flick. No light. The presence was controlling the light. I fumbled with the door handle and pulled the door open. A silhouette of Mum greeted me in the darkness of the hall, making me jump.

'Get... back... in ... bed!' Mum growled.

I retreated, with nowhere left to turn but back to my bed in the pitch dark room. I wrapped the covers around my head and listened to every single sound, small or great, which bumped or creaked in the flat, daring not to sneak even a single peek just in case I should see the thing that was in my room, menacing and oppressive, causing terror and pinning me down on the bed.

After drifting off into an uneasy sleep I woke up and again jumped out of bed, sprinting for the light switch. This time the light came on. The room was empty and the presence had diminished. I counted to three and switched the light back off before making a dash back to my bed.

Mum became less and less concerned about how I felt and the flat felt less and less like home. I would get an uneasy feeling on the way home from school, especially on dark and cloudy days. If it was light and sunny outside, I could feel happy about life. It may have been that Mum felt happier when it was sunny too, I cannot say for sure. Even now when I think about that hilarious cartoon Danger Mouse, it gives me a feeling of sadness, a feeling that all is not quite right. It was part of that routine, of stepping on eggshells whilst trying not to crunch them underfoot and wake the sleeping dog that was Mum's low moods and angry attacks. Things became even worse when Mum found a friend to give her emotional support – Calvin's mum.

Calvin's mum was kind to me mostly and I liked her at first, even though I knew some of what she did to Calvin. I hung around a lot with Calvin, even though he was not part of my main friendship group at school. He was in my class but hardly attended. Calvin's mum beat him a lot. I think that's why we got on with one another so well; we understood each other. He showed me his sore marks, which were much worse and far more frequent than mine. I showed him mine – small wounds compared to his. He would tell me what his mum used to beat him with – the flex from the kettle, washing line, a stick. One day Calvin came in to school with a black eye, telling everybody that he had been fighting with 'an idiot'. He later told me that his mum had beaten him and thumped him in the face. Calvin's mum actually punched him.

I remember the last time I went round to his

house to play. Calvin's mum let us in after school. She stood in the hall smiling at us both with her big brown eyes from behind her round glasses. She was young and pretty, wearing a skirt and sandals with her dark hair plaited close to her head.

'Would you boys like some milkshake? What flavour would you like Dominic? We have chocolate, strawberry, banana...'

'Banana please.'

'Calvin?'

'Strawberry.'

'Strawberry what?'

'Please.'

Off she disappeared into the kitchen, and returned with two huge glasses full of milkshake, both banana.

'No more strawberry I'm afraid Calvin. You've used it all up.'

We played in Calvin's room that day. He showed me his poster of a woman playing tennis. She was walking towards the net with a racket in one hand, whilst her other hand was holding her bare bottom cheek. I was shocked that Calvin was allowed to have this picture on his wall. Calvin laughed and laughed at me whilst I sat looking at his poster, slurping my milkshake. Then there was a knock on the bedroom door and Calvin's mum came in.

'Calvin, it's time for your friend to leave now. Say hi to Mary for me Dominic. Tell her I'll see her soon.'

The whole atmosphere in Calvin's flat had changed. His mum looked cross with him, pursing her lips as she ushered me out. Calvin was still smiling but he had a downcast look in his eyes. As I walked down the steps and out of the block, I heard the shouting and screaming begin already.

Mum and Calvin's mum had become friends. Mum would talk about her as if she were Mum's mentor in all things related to discipline and parenting. Mum would tell me what they had discussed, what they both agreed on and what they had in common.

'She says I need to keep control of you. She's a single mum and she knows what she's talking about. She understands how it's been for me over the years with you. She understands.'

If Mum was particularly angry, she would compare me with Calvin.

'He doesn't even do half of the things that you do. He's a lovely lad. I feel sorry for him because he gets beaten sometimes when he doesn't even deserve it. Not like you. You should get what he gets from his mum. Is that what you want, eh? You think you get beaten? You think I beat you properly? Well I might start doing it properly if you don't buck up your ideas.'

When Calvin just disappeared one day, everybody was saying that he had been taken into care because his mum had beaten him so badly, that he was in a children's home now. It was hard to think that Calvin had been so badly beaten, that he might be injured. I missed him after he disappeared. He was so funny and battle-hardened, and kind. But at the same time I was glad for him that he was not living at home any more, glad that he was not getting beaten by his mum.

I told my mum what had happened to Calvin with relish. For me it was proof that other grownups did not think it was okay for a child to be beaten like that. It was proof to me that what Mum was doing to me was wrong and I knew that seeing the evidence before her of other people's disapproval would cause her to think again, and to find another way to be a mother.

Mum's response, however, was devastating.

'He pushed her too far. She couldn't cope with him anymore. That's what will happen to you if you don't change your ways.'

In Mum's mind, Calvin had been punished not rescued. It was a blueprint for our relationship, based on our own history and now confirmed by her friend's plight. The ultimate sanction for being bad was to be taken into care. This would happen when Mum could no longer cope with my bad behaviour. It was to be the rescue package for Mum when I was way, way too hard to handle.

But it would not be a rescue package for me.

When I first arrived in Brixton from Jamaica, I had hope for me and Mum. We would wander around the colourful Brixton Market and buy beef patties and Hardo bread from the open counter shop on the corner. We would stand and gaze up as Mum would tell me about the giant mural outside the back entrance to Brixton Market. The mural was called

'Nuclear Dawn' and had a giant white skeleton dressed in American, British, and Russian flags. The bony herald with the hollow eyes stood astride London, with his foot crashing into Westminster as he straddled the River Thames. Behind the skeleton billowed a glowing double mushroom cloud filled with screaming faces. In the bottom corner a huddle of politicians were exposed in their wrecked bunker. Mum would tell me who all the corrupt politicians were. She even took me to a 'Ban the Bomb' rally in Hyde Park once, and we sat on the grass listening to Tony Benn.

Then we would march up the road together to 'The Front Line' where Mum would disappear with a man with long dreadlocks whilst I would stand and stare at the goodies in the window of the 'red, gold and green' shop which sold everything from T-shirts to sweat bands to lighters, so long as they had the right colours. Then, after Mum had scored her weed, we would nip into the earthy-smelling health food shop where Mum would buy a piece of carrot cake to share. We would stop at every single cat on the way home, and Mum would crouch and put her hand out making cat noises like she did, and every cat would come and nuzzle against her hand and wind its body and swish its tail between her legs as I tried to get a few strokes in myself.

It was good between us at first. Mum started out happy in London with me. We went to festivals in the local parks together. We listened to reggae music side by side, either standing right next to the mammoth speakers, or sitting on the grass eating Caribbean takeaway. At first it had been good when it was just me and her in the sunshine.

At the same time Mum used to play a really depressing song to me, as if it could somehow cheer us both up. 'Let me take you by the hand and lead you through the streets of London. I'll show you something that will make you change your mind.' In London, Mum's mind did seem to change but not in a good way. She became unreachable to me, distant and unavailable. As we finally moved out of Heman's Estate in the wake of the bulldozers, it felt like the remains of my relationship with Mum had also been knocked down. I felt like her enemy, her problem, her biggest letdown.

As much as I hated the darkness of the small flat, watching my old home being knocked down that way felt cataclysmic.

It felt like the end of the world.

The day we moved into Waldon Court on the other side of Wandsworth Road, I felt a flicker of new hope. Mum was round with Eli's baby and it was a new start, a new nest. There was a new and brighter view from my third-floor bedroom window. When I went to the top of the ten storey block I could see all over London – Big Ben, the Post Office Tower and soul-warming sunsets behind Battersea Power Station. We all started well in Waldon Court and when my eldest sister was born the spotlight was off me – which was good.

Mum coped amazingly well with the challenges of

caring for and feeding a newborn baby. I helped where I could, doing shopping and extra cleaning and staying off school. I would carry two huge boxes of Pampers nappies, which were half my size, all the way back from Mother Care. I tripped over once and fell flat on my face, still holding the two purple boxes. My little sister was amazing. She would sit in her cot, rubbing a silky yellow blanket on her face, holding her cuddly toy – Jemima Puddle-Duck – in her other hand. Her eyelids would droop as she fell asleep for her afternoon nap and I felt warm. There was love in my house once again.

But it wasn't long before all that changed.

It was in the afternoon at the weekend. I was reading in my room when I heard a loud bang.

'Police! Open the door, Mary, open up. Open the door right now!'

There was another bang.

Mum flew into my room with two round cakes of hash wrapped in cling film. She opened my window, looked up and down, and then dropped them one by one into the bushes at the foot of the block.

Bang. Bang.

'When I give you the signal, go and pick them up, put them under your jumper, and take them around to George's house. Tell him to keep them for me and tell him we got a raid.'

Bang. Bang. Crash.

I nodded.

The door creaked on its hinges and the sound of wood cracking filled the un-carpeted flat as police officers poured in. Some went this way, some went that way. One sat down with Mum, who was by now cradling my sister who was crying and crying.

'Look what you've done to my door, you dutty babylon. You aint gonna find nothing in my flat. You got a warrant? Show me your warrant.'

'Mary, Mr Tailor has been detained on suspicion of importing drugs into the UK.'

Mum suddenly fell silent and looked at the officer. Then she began to cry.

'Where is he? What have you done with him?'

'He has been arrested and detained in Wales.'

'Where is he, you pig?'

'Mary, he's in Wales. Now, are you keeping any drugs on the premises, Mary? We are going to conduct a full house search. What are we going to find here?'

Mum gave me a look and I slinked off, leaving police officers emptying drawers and moving furniture around.

Eli was gone. Mum, my sister, and I were now alone. I took Mum's two hash cakes round to her friend's, no doubt being followed by the police. Eli was gone. Why was he in Wales? I knew he had been working away a lot, but why Wales of all places? I walked back with an empty jumper and an empty feeling inside.

Eli was gone.

*

Mum was stronger now after recovering from the birth. She was fit enough to deal with me but I had grown bigger. We didn't dance any more. Mum flew at me in a rage, lashing with the belt or the flex, the kettle flex. It hurt my hands and arms but the blows rarely got through to my legs, or torso, or head.

'This would all be over much quicker if you just let me give you what you know is coming to you. The more you flap around with your hands the more time it takes, right?'

Then an idea flickered behind her green eyes. I wanted her eyes to look at me and adore me, to see me again, but they glinted with cold inspiration. She had thought of a new way to make sure I got exactly what I deserved.

'You are going to put your hands on the bed and I am going to tie them to the bed.'

I could not believe my ears. This is what Calvin's mum used to do to him. I wanted to laugh out loud but I didn't. It seemed unreal. Mum disappeared and soon returned, much calmer now, with a length of washing line from the bathroom.

'Put your hands at the end of your bed and let me tie you up.'

Mum was not joking. I smiled. I couldn't help it.

'Don't you smirk at me, you little swine. Put your hands on the bed.'

'No Mum. If I do that, you'll hit me.'

'Yes, but only three times. If you let me get three good licks on your legs then it'll be over. Do you understand? You are getting proper discipline even if it takes me all night. Just put your hands on the bed and I promise it will only be three.'

I did it. I did what Mum was asking me to do without resistance. I put my hands on the bed and Mum wrapped the line round and around my wrists, weaving under and over, in and out. As Mum secured both my hands to the bed frame, we both knelt down together. I could feel her warm breath on my face. I could smell her perfume. Her arms rubbed against mine as she tied the last knots, skin on skin. I felt close to her.

I had decided to put my trust in her. Mum had offered me a measured amount of discipline. She had calmed down and she had made a rational choice. Maybe she was doing this because she loved me, because she just wanted me to turn out right. Maybe this was her caring for me. As she was so close to me and calm; it almost felt like Mum was caring for me again.

Only three.

I could take three.

Then it would be over.

Mum stood and I watched her over my shoulder. I barely moved as the first swipe bore down on me but as it hit I jumped because it hurt. I could not help but flinch and wriggle for the second and third. The kettle flex hurt and Mum was using her full force. The end was thick and heavy and it swung well because of the extra weight. When number four came down the deal was off and my hands began to strain and pull as the line dug into my wrists. Then I lost count. I wriggled my hands and kicked my legs, my back exposed to Mum's discipline. Eventually the line loosened and I sprang up onto my feet, my back stinging.

'What are you doing Mum? What do you think you're doing?'

I stood panting with my back to the corner of the room, looking at Mum who was smirking at me. She didn't look like Mum. She was small but menacing, with dark eyes with no spark of love in them. The flex hung at her side, still gripped by one of her clenched fists.

I never again gave myself over to be tied to the bed. Hands that once held me as I bobbed in the water at Queen Street Baths now tightened into fists that punched and hit, whilst I crouched, trying to protect my face and ears.

Mum was strong for such a small woman and punching became the new beating.

She was becoming more and more like Calvin's mum. Just like the lover in Paul Simon's song 'Fifty ways to leave your lover', I felt Mum begin to whisper the list of them to me.

# 23

# FATHERS

'Maurice Morton, Youth Club leader at Springfield Methodist Church is well known to Dominic. Miss White's co-habitee is in prison. The main trouble is mother is planning to return to Jamaica and Dominic does not want this.'

'Mary.'

'Ted Burrows.'

'Derby.'

Note on back of RIC paperwork from Lambeth, written by Receiving Officer on 23rd February 1985.

*

Eli left Mum with a parting gift, her second daughter. As Mum grew round again we went up and down on the train to Wales where Eli was facing his trial for attempting to import a container full of cannabis from Jamaica. Consequently I began to miss more and more of my first year at Stockwell Manor Secondary School. A seven year sentence came as a shock to Mum and Eli. I looked at my sweet little sister with her big brown eyes and fuzzy dark hair, knowing that she would hardly see her dad. Since Mum had discovered that she was pregnant again, her rages had calmed down and become much less frequent. With Eli gone, life became more about survival and making ends meet. Scales were kept in the kitchen as people came to Mum's shop to sample and buy dark brown hash, or golden temple balls, or pungent sensimilla. There were always a couple of plants around, standing in pots under a large lamp. Mum would water them and talk to them softly.

Income was supplemented by benefits from the Social Services and from interest from a lump of money sitting in the bank. Me, Mum, and my sister would walk to the bank in Brixton and she would withdraw whatever interest there was for that month. Mum eventually explained our financial situation to me, in part at least.

'My mum left you some money. It should have come to me. I was just borrowing it so that I could make it grow.'

'You mean the three-and-a-half thousand pounds Grandma left to me?'

'Yes.'

'I thought I couldn't have that until I was eighteen years old.'

'Well, that was sort of true. It was left with me and your dad to look after for you. We went to the Building Society and signed it out.'

'What, Ted and you?'

'Yes. If the Babylon hadn't taken it, we would have been rich. Dem burn it all up Dougie, set fire to the whole ting.'

'Set fire to the money?'

'No darling. The weed. Dem burn it, destroyed the lot. Destroyed your inheritance.'

'You mean you used my money to buy the weed from Jamaica?'

'It wasn't just your money. It was our money, the whole family's.'

'So is it all gone now then? Won't I get any of it when I'm eighteen?'

'There's some left, about one thousand pounds, but I'm trying to save that.'

'Is that what you get the interest from?'

'Yes.'

Mum had met up with Ted whilst I was at Birdcage Walk. She had withdrawn my trust fund with Ted's signed consent and then gone shopping with it in Jamaica. She had bought a family airfare return, a six month working holiday, and a large shipping container full of mango tins, which were not full of mangos. My mind jumped back to Nottingham, to the plush flat, to Mum's level of peace and contentment. Things could have been the same again if only the police hadn't found the container full of my inheritance.

Eventually we stopped going to the bank. Money became tight and Mum became very creative. I had a pair of blue roller boots with yellow rainbow stripes, just like everybody else. I would skate and skate all around Landsdown Green Estate and up to Brixton Skate Park and back again. Mum now received a school clothing grant. We bought some blue shirts, a tie and a pair of trousers. The same shop also sold school blazers and roller boots. We chose the roller boots. Later, when I stood in the second-hand shop trying the brown donkey jacket on, I felt confident. Mum was smiling at me. The lady said it was a nice fit. When I turned up at school with it they destroyed me. That was the last time I wore a blazer, or a donkey jacket, at Stockwell Manor. But I loved my skates.

Then there was Mum's marijuana shop. There was always something cooking in her kitchen. Heavy, sweet smells filled the flat as hot knives cut through thick black cakes which were weighed and wrapped in cling film. Pungent bags of green leaves and stalk were weighed, burnt and rolled up in liquorice cigarette papers.

As Eli was now in prison doing a seven-year stretch, Mum decided to take me to the church over the road to get a 'religious education' - something she valued a lot, surprisingly. She almost dragged me over there one Sunday morning, while I resisted as much as I dared. It felt like a punishment. As it turned out, Mum deciding to draw upon the church to help to bring me up worked out well for me. It gave me access to substitute father figures.

But church was not the only place where Mum sought out father figures on my behalf. The man with the machine gun strapped across his shoulder was a wild card, even by our standards.

*

John was tall, athletic and craggy-looking with a mop of dirty blonde hair. When he had his machine gun in his hands, he looked like he was going to kill someone until he smiled at me and ruffled my hair.

'How's the kid, Mary?'

'Fine, he's fine.'

John had a friend – a shorter, darker haired man who also carried a machine gun. He didn't smile so much so I didn't talk to him. John was funny and calm. The two men came to the flat down the hall almost every day but didn't live there. They would knock on our door and I would stand in the corridor talking to John while Mum went and got the bags of white stuff for them. Mum stashed it for them so that John and his friend were safe when they were selling it in their flat. John told me that it came off the ship, went to a man and then came to him. It was very expensive so they paid Mum a little bit of money to keep it safe for them.

'Why do you have guns then?'

'So we can shoot rabbits for tea, son.'

'Do you eat rabbits?'

'Yeah, for breakfast.'

John let me touch his machine gun once because I asked him. It was black, with a strap that hung it from John's shoulder. The metal was cold and smooth to the touch.

This was a happier time for Mum. She seemed more herself again for a short while. John was always sniffing and wiping his nose, and Mum started to do this more often as well.

One night Mum told me all about the white powder in our flat.

'It's called coke. Or cocaine.'

'Do you take any, Mum?'

'Yeah, a little bit.'

'Is it like smoking weed?'

'No, no. It's totally different. It's like someone switches the light bulb on in your head. Your thoughts come at one hundred miles an hour and it's like you can see everything a lot clearer. Everything clicks into place.'

Sometimes John seemed disappointed with Mum but never with me. Mum was doing something that she shouldn't be doing and John said, "I told you not to Mary. If you keep doing this our arrangement will have to stop."

Even though Mum was cutting into what did not belong to her, John didn't hold any of this against me personally.

'Mary, when was the last time this kid went on a holiday? He's got to have some fun you know. He's a growing lad. Can I take him on holiday down South with me, Mary?'

I looked at John and at Mum and back to John. A smile broke across my face and my eyes began to plead. I thought that I had better ask, just for show.

'Where will it be to?'

I didn't actually care.

'Well, we'll go down to our flat in Hastings for a bit

and then we'll spend a week or two at our house in Sevenoaks in Kent.'

'And who else is going?'

I didn't really care. I would be happy so long as John was going.

'It will be you, me, my girlfriend, and her sister.'

'Okay. Can I go Mum? Please?'

Not longer after I was in another world – ice cream on Hastings beach, sitting on the shingle with John while the two girls went swimming; sleeping in the flat while John and his girlfriend argued about how much coke he was using; walking along the beach talking to the girl with the light brown skin and dental braces. John's house in Sevenoaks was an absolute palace, with a massive garden to match. There was a huge oak tree at the bottom of the garden with a swing. Me and 'Braces' took it in turns to push each other as we laughed and played and explored all day long. There was a huge fridge full of food and drinks and meals lasted ages, eaten on the patio as the sun lowered itself in the sky and the heat of the day lifted.

My holiday with John ended too soon when the girl and I were put on a London-bound train. We rattled and swayed through the night as the cool evening breeze swept in through the open windows at the top. I had got to know the girl fairly well over those weeks and she had begun to feel like an older sister. I wanted her to tell me that she would see me again some other time as she got off once the train had gone over the Thames, but she didn't. I knew that I would never see her again. I only had the one holiday with John the dealer and his girlfriend and her sister, but it was one of the best holidays I had ever had.

*

When John stopped coming to our flat, Mum's mind turned back to Derby. At some point during the summer of 1983 when I was twelve, Mum sent me alone on a train back to Derby for a day to find my dad. She made a phone call, checked the departure times and prices, and wrote me two notes. The notes were given to me in sealed envelopes, accompanied by a hand drawn map of some roads and streets in Derby.

'Don't you dare open these letters. I will know if you have opened them.'

'I won't.'

The fact that Mum was financing the expedition was a big thing for me. It was all about me finding my father. Yes, I had been going to church. Yes, I had become friendly with M&M who ran the youth club and Sunday School. I had even been on holiday a few times with them to 'The Cottage' where they took all of us London kids so that we could experience the deep silence of darkest Oxfordshire. But despite M&M, and John, and the less and less frequent visits to Eli, Mum still wanted me to find my own dad, and that really meant something to me.

The two letters were the start of my confusion. The instructions were to go and find Ted at Albion Taxis and give him the first letter. Then I was to go either with Ted or on my own to a chip shop just outside Derby and hand over the second letter. When I asked Mum about the chip shop, she told me there was a chance that Ted was not my real dad and that the people in the chip shop might know where I could find my real dad.

My *real* dad!

This was the first time I had heard Mum talk about my real dad. Just knowing that Ted might not be my dad gave me all the determination I needed to take Mum's money, and the letters and the map, and to board the Derby-bound train.

My memory of the trip is hazy. The honest truth is that I cannot remember if I saw Ted or not. I have half a memory which says that there was a panic and a fluster when I presented the letter to the control room. Ted, who had been retired for some time, was called in. In one version he turned up, told me he was not my dad, then left. In another, he never turned up and I left. In any event, I did leave the taxi waiting room without him. Then I set off following the instructions on Mum's hand-crafted map to the mysterious chip shop, tightly grasping the second letter. This is the bit that I do remember, with crystal clarity.

When I arrived at the chip shop, it was open but empty. I entered and put my letter and my hands on the counter whilst I looked at the food in the hot cabinet beside me, and the lady behind the counter. She looked Turkish, or maybe Greek, and wore a headscarf out of which curls of dark hair fell.

'What can I get you darling?'

I pushed the letter towards her. 'I don't want any chips. My mum sent me with this and told me to bring it here and give it to you.'

The lady's eyes looked at me and then down at the letter. I picked it up and held it out to her. Eventually she took it while calling through the bead curtains behind her. She opened the letter as a man and another lady came through the curtains. She read it and passed it on. She looked at me silently then went behind the beads. The man and the other lady stood and read it, then looked at me. Then they told me to wait and disappeared behind the beads leaving me and the fried battered fish alone. There were voices and then silence. I wanted to know what they were talking about, to know what Mum had written in the letter.

Eventually the man came out and spoke to me in broken English. He had an angry look on his face.

'You not come back here. You tell your Mum, no father is here. You must leave now.'

I didn't argue. I wanted to ask him to give me the letter back but I didn't.

On the way back to the train station, I asked a young couple what the time was as I was anxious about missing my train. The man replied smugly, 'Time you got a watch.' Emotion consumed me and I lost it. I swore at the man with everything I could muster, all the foulest words I could remember. All of my anger and frustration poured out onto that smug man. He walked on, still laughing with his girlfriend.

'All I wanted was the time. Just the time, that's all. Is that too much to ask? Is it? Is it?'

When I was thirty-seven years old I bought my first personal mobile phone. It had a camera on it which I used to take a photo of myself so that I could send it to my mum. She sent me a text back saying, 'I know who your father is'. I called her.

'I know who he is now. You remember that waiter we used to see in Derby?'

'Yeah.'

'It's him. His name is Harry Cristos, with no 'h' in Cristos. He's your dad.'

'How do you know for sure?'

'It's your hairline. He's your dad. It's not Ted, it's definitely him.'

I asked question after question after question. Suddenly Mum was ready to talk about the unspoken mystery which had always hung over my paternal origins. I didn't want to let the moment slip. I took down names and streets and names of Greek-Cypriot restaurants.

'Athena. Or maybe Apollo. I think his dad had two Greek restaurants.'

Mum's eyes were green. Ted's eyes were grey. My eyes are brown. I looked at my own two girls with their brown eyes and olive skin. They had Harry's eyes. I understood that eye colour was not conclusive proof but somehow I knew. Suddenly something about my identity just clicked into place as I sat looking at the phone in the kitchen. It was like when Sarah reminded me on Facebook that my grandma used to call me her Prince. Something I had lost returned to me. I knew his name – his name. I knew he was Greek-Cypriot and that I shared in his heritage. I knew he had brown eyes. I knew he was my father. But in 1983 I did not know this and so I came back from Derby on the train feeling crushed.

*

Sometimes Mum would give me a five pound note at tea time.

'Go over to Georgina's café and tell them Mary sent you.'

The café was two minutes walk away along the Wandsworth Road. I would always order moussaka and banana milkshake. Everyone in Georgina's Café was olive-skinned with dark hair and rounded Mediterranean accents. Mum told me that they would feed me well and they did. She told me that they would look after me and make me feel at home, which they did.

I thought about the lady's smile all the way there. I stood and watched as she poured the Crusha syrup into the glass and then added milk. If I ran out of milkshake and they were not too busy they would give me a free top up. I tried to make the moussaka last as long as possible as I watched the serious-looking man serve customers and cook food and shoot me a wink every now and again. I sat and looked at the framed pictures hanging on the walls, pictures of beaches and island maps, and a city with towers and spires glinting in the sun. I ate the aubergine and meat and potato with cheese and white sauce. It felt more like visiting an uncle and aunty's house than eating tea alone in a greasy-spoon café.

The woman came to get my empty plate as I finished my milkshake. She stopped and rocked back on one hip looking at me with a smiling frown.

'You have Greek parents, Dominic?'

'No, my dad was an English taxi driver.'

'You sure?'

'I think so.'

'Well, you look Greek to me, at least half anyway. And you eat so much moussaka.'

'I like your moussaka.'

I am still looking for Harry.

I want to see his eyes.

*

Another man whom Mum thought might have a positive influence on me was Major. Major ran a shop from his flat on the Angel Town estate where I spent one of the weirdest nights in my life.

I knew Mum smoked cannabis and Mum knew I did not want to smoke it myself. Mum was a great believer in the properties of the herb and wished me to partake, or at least show a desire to do so, so she took me to Major's house. When we arrived, we were both shown to the fish tank by a short, muscular man with shoulder-length dreadlocks.

'You have to choose a fish. Then you have to swallow the fish. Then you get de life-force of it inside-a unuh.'

Mum chose a goldfish. In her mouth it went, followed by gulps of water from a glass. Then it was my turn. I chose the smallest goldfish I could lay my eyes on.

'No bother chewing the fish. It has to go down whole and alive.'

'Does it wriggle?'

'A little in your mouth, but once it's down you don't feel a thing.'

The fish was pulled out in a net and plopped out into a shallow amount of water in a pint glass which was handed to me. Another pint glass full of water was on hand.

'Pop it in and knock it back now!' His red eyes glinted at me as I watched him, and then the fish, and then him again.

In it went with all the water. It flipped against my tongue and cheeks. I swallowed hard, again and again, grabbing the second pint glass and knocking back as much water as I could – gulp after gulp, just to get the fish moving down until at last there was peace in my throat. This was followed by a spliff. And another spliff. And another. Most of the night was spent sitting on the sofa watching people come and go through the balcony curtains as Major danced barefoot to loud reggae music. I sat talking to Joe who told me about Marxism and Trotsky and how he was studying sociology and politics at university. All of this washed over me as I became distracted by the fact that my tongue was rubbing against the roof of my mouth.

Then Joe, Major and I went on a 'mission'. First we drove in a car with me in the back and a bucket full of Major's excrement and urine in the boot. Major drove the car around the edge of estates unfamiliar to me. Every so often Joe would jump out of the car and take the bucket from the boot. Then he would splash some of it up against a wall whilst the blocks full of sleeping people towered above us. I mustered a question as Major and I sat with the engine running, waiting for Joe to return.

'Major, why.... do you.... do that?'

'It's like a dog marking his territory. You have to keep your enemies off your area.'

'So it's like a dog then.'

'Just like a dog, only I couldn't sit and do de ting in the street to ras!'

'No, to ras!'

Then we parked the car up and took a short tube journey on the London Underground.

'It helps get rid of my wind, all the shaking and bumping. Look here, you better try this, see? Hold on and stretch out your ribs like this.' Major and Joe both hung from the handrails with their feet pulled up from the floor, arms and bodies fully outstretched.

'See, give it a try!' There followed an audible rumble heard even above the rattle of the tube train followed by peals of laughter and noxious odours from all three of us who thankfully were the only passengers in the tube carriage.

By the time we returned to Angel Town it was getting light and as soon as we entered Major's patio doors he disappeared into the kitchen to make cornmeal porridge. Eating this thick, tasty sweet food was the best way to end possibly the craziest night of my life. It tasted authentically Jamaican, just like Granny used to make.

Although it had not been the worst night of my life, it was way too unusual for me to ever want to repeat it, so in the end Mum's plan to acclimatise me to ganja backfired. But I must give credit to Joe, whoever he was, for taking me under his wing and looking after me, and to Major for his amazing cornmeal porridge.

*

After my second sister was born at the end of 1983, Mum took a turn for the worse. Once she had recovered physically from the birth, the beatings started again. I tried to help as much as I could around the house, and was often taking time off school to help Mum with shopping, or with the girls. Looking after two toddlers and a teenage boy single-handed must have been hard for Mum. Yet she tried.

As I was missing so much school, Mum bought

me some second-hand books to read at home – a green Bible, Homer's Iliad, and The Hobbit and Lord of the Rings. I was made to read through the first three chapters of Genesis and write notes for Mum to prove I had read it. Then I read part way through The Iliad but could not finish it. But as soon as I picked up The Hobbit I was hooked. It was something that Mum and I now had in common. She loved Tolkien and she read one book whilst I was reading the other. I spent hours and days reading, roller-skating, running errands, eating at Georgina's Café, and getting into trouble again with Mum.

The dynamic was diluted with two happy-go-lucky toddlers running around the place but Mum was just asking too much of me. I still couldn't be who she wanted me to be. I still found it so hard to do things that consistently pleased her. I was too big now to beat with a belt or a flex; I would just grab it and hold it. Mum pulled my hair and spat at me and punched me. Another means of discipline was banning me from attending church or youth club. I had become close to M&M over the last year or so having spent a few holidays with them at 'The Cottage' and often eating Sunday lunch with them in their flat at the top of the Methodist church.

'Right, that's it. You're not going on holiday with them and you're not going to youth club either. You're banned for a week.'

'You're banned for two weeks.'

'You're not going there ever again. They're trying to brainwash you.'

On 31st May 1984 I was once again received into care, this time for a few months. Four days later on the 4th June 1984 I started at a new school – the Archbishop Michael Ramsay School in Camberwell – and attended almost every day from my temporary foster placement in Coldharbour Lane. I still visited Mum and my sisters but only at the weekends. Mum had decided to drop me off one day at Social Services because she could no longer cope with my bad behaviour. Eventually Mum took me out of care again and things just took off from where we had left them. I was glad to be back with her in October 1984 because I had missed my sisters and the familiarity of home.

I remember exactly what Mum bought me for Christmas in December 1984. It was a pencil case with a maths set in it for my new school, and a peaked 'disco hat' with lights in it that I could wear whilst I was roller skating. I was devastated at the time but looking back they were actually quite thoughtful presents.

In January 1985 everything changed. Mum was excited. She had had a phone call and was expecting a visitor.

'Go over the road and get me a bottle of Bells whisky. He likes Bells. Tell the shopkeeper that Mary sent you and that the drink is for me. And ask him for a big paper bag'

I bought the whisky which Mum wrapped in the large paper bag.

'Take this and go on the bus to Victoria Coach

Station. When you see him, give him the bottle and say that Mary sent it. It's his favourite.'

'Whose favourite, Mum?'

'You'll recognise him when you see him. It's Duke, Dougie, it's Duke. He's coming to stay with us. Isn't that great?'

# 24

# THE OTHER WORLD

The big man stretched out as he stepped off the coach and looked around. I walked up to him, holding out the bottle.

'Hello Duke, I'm Mary's son. She sent you this.'

Duke whacked his hand on my back and beamed a huge smile at me as he took the bottle and pulled off the paper bag.

'What you sending me, Mary? Whisky? Bells? She knows me well Dominic. Your mother knows me full well.'

He put the paper bag back around the bottle and broke open the top before taking a swig. He then pushed the bottle towards me.

'You want to try a bit?'

'Yeah, okay.' I thought it would be rude not to. I took a small swig and swallowed the warm liquid. He swigged all the way back on the bus as I looked longingly for a second helping of the warming fluid, but none was offered.

I had been sent at night with whisky to bring him back. I was the one who guided him back into our home. Mum had sent me, her son, to greet the love of her life – the big man who liked saunas and counting money – and fighting with Mum.

She was once again quickly besotted with the big Jamaican man. Duke still had that effect upon her. The first night he stayed I had a pounding headache. Mum said it was the gas fires but I felt groggy and strange with it. I tried to stay up, sitting on the floor at the end of Mum's bed, but eventually I crawled to my own bed and left them play-fighting under the covers.

Mum and Duke started going out together. This was fine with me because it was usually in the evening or at night when the girls were asleep and I would be reading, sleeping or watching telly. Mum and Duke would go out in the afternoon and return in the morning. When they were at home, Duke hardly came out of the bedroom and Mum's life became focussed on serving him and attending to his needs. It wasn't long before Duke began to go out on his own.

It was not like Mum to drink but when Duke was living with us at Waldon Court, she drank. She drank when Duke was in and when Duke was out. Reggae music would be playing loud into the night, often keeping me awake. Yes, Mum had changed since Duke was back on the scene, but that wasn't the real problem. I wonder sometimes exactly how Mum and Duke got back in touch with each other. Did Mum write him a letter, or did he write to her? There was no Internet or Facebook or mobile phones for the masses back in 1985. Communication was not as free-flowing as it is today. But was it Duke that changed everything? I'm not sure it was.

Maybe it was how things were changing between Mum and I. With age I had become less compliant and perhaps a bit rude at times. We still had our fun moments together from time to time, even at that lowest ever point of our relationship. Like the time I decided to cut my own fringe – just a little snip this way. Now it just needs straightening – just a little snip the other way, zigzag, up and up, rising up my forehead until I looked like I had given myself a very bad haircut, which I had. Mum found this hilarious and her fits of laughter eventually rubbed off on me and she helped me to straighten it out. Or the times we would walk all the way to Battersea Park together with the two buggies filled with my two beautiful and lively sisters and their bottles and snacks. We would feed the ducks and wander around the flowerbeds and pathways until the cool of the evening. The girls were always happy on the way home, quietly worn out and watching the world pass by as their dummies sucked in and out behind the yellow veil of comfort blankets that softly rubbed their cheeks.

Yes, Mum still hit me but I was at that age when for a boy strength grows and height increases in leaps and bounds. I was bigger than Mum now and a little stronger, even then. There was one time, just one time, when I nearly lost it with Mum. We were in the hall and Mum was a little drunk and very angry. She was crying and punching and snarling at me. I grabbed her hands and pinned them to her sides in a misjudged attempt to try and calm her down. She spat full in my face – in my mouth, and in my eyes. My fists clenched as I stood in front of her.

'Go on then, hit me if you want. Hit me and see what happens, you little shit. Go on...' Mum had stopped screaming and flailing and stood still in front of me with her eyes blazing and spittle flying at every word.

'Don't you ever square up to me. You haven't even got what it takes.'

*I have never had anything it takes in your book. This time you might be wrong.*

Everything in me wanted to hit her. Just once. I could smell her spit on my face and taste it in my mouth. I felt sick. We stood facing each other in silence, Mum putting all of her energy into staring me down and me shaking with anger, fists still clenched. My whole arm wanted to make the movement, to knock her out stone cold on the ground like Adam had done to me. Everything in me. Everything in me.

But I didn't.

My fists unclenched and my eyes finally fell to the floor. I wiped the spit off my face and went into the bathroom to brush my teeth. That was the last time Mum ever punched me. Or spat at me. This was where we had come to – a mistrustful, hate-filled stalemate. And the hatred was now beginning to flow both ways.

I tried to be around in the kitchen as much as I could when Mum was cooking in a bad mood. I began to imagine that she was spitting in my food and mixing it in, or poisoning it. There was hardly any clear air between us towards the end so I stayed out as much as I could, or in my room reading, or practising my guitar. I withdrew from family life as much as I possibly could too. I didn't dislike Duke as such but I did dislike the effect he had on Mum. One day Mum was up in the heights of dizzying happiness; the next day her world was falling apart because he had left, or they had argued. When he came back he acted as if he had popped to the shops. Nothing to complain about here, just move along and get back to where we all were before I vanished for three days.

All of Mum's time was now being taken away from me and directed at Duke and the girls. I began to feel just like Walter the Lazy Mouse, left behind and forgotten. Hatred and resentment grew in me. For the first time ever, I began to become the darker one. This time it was me who began looking for a way out.

*

My first visit to the Cottage had been in August 1982. Between that first time and August 1984 it is recorded in the visitor's book that I went there six times and I know there were other times which were not recorded. We would go up to Uffington White Horse and the Hill Fort. M&M would drop us off at Dragon Hill where we would clamber out of the minibus and leap up the mound. On the top lies a bare patch of chalk where no grass ever grows – a patch of earth scorched forever by the slain dragon's blood. Then we would run down one side of The Manger, and crawl back up the other to meet M&M on the high plain. We would fly kites and roll around and drink in the huge vista of The Vale as the clouds raced by overhead. It's the same place that Kate Bush made her video for her song 'Cloud-busting'. When I travelled to Eli's trial in Wales I could see the White Horse from the window as the train sped by between Oxford and Swindon. I always looked out for the chalk figure, far off in the distance.

Mum wanted me to be a drug dealer. She spoke of it in terms of 'the family business', knowing that it would wind me up and make me defensive. I was inadequate as a dealer. I didn't have any of what it takes according to Mum. Her opinion was that even if I didn't like it myself because of all that brainwashing the people at church had done to me, I could at least help her out a bit. There came a point where I refused to run errands for her anymore. I would not carry hash or weed from A to B and I would not help her to get her money back from people who owed her. I was increasingly opting out and Mum hated it.

I had been granted a taste of a good education at Archbishop Michael Ramsay School and loved it. It wasn't that Stockwell Manor had been a bad school; it was more that I had been a bad pupil, missing way too many lessons and days. I had needed a fresh start, which Mrs Cohen – the Education Welfare Officer – had won for me. I liked English, Biology, Geography and Art. I had been on field trips to Wales and climbed the mountain in one of my favourite books by Susan Cooper, *The Grey King*. I had been to the top of Cader Idris itself and camped by the mountain lake on the other side. Mum wanted us all to return to Jamaica, not for a long holiday this time, but forever. I didn't want to live in Jamaica forever; I wanted to stay here.

I had grown to love M&M who had no children of their own but loved me, along with all the other kids on the estate who came to their clubs and Oxfordshire holidays. They had a flat that smelled like home, and a cat, and a cottage in the countryside. We would all go for walks together down the lane and into the fields and on and on. Eventually we would reach the train line where we would wait for a train to swish by as we waved. Sometimes the driver would wave back and toot his blower at us. This was the same train that took me and Mum and my eldest sister to Cardiff and back, past the Uffington White Horse.

It was hard living with Mum and refusing to get involved in her entrepreneurial activities. I couldn't keep standing up to her and defending my position. I couldn't explain clearly enough who I was and who I wasn't. By now I had experienced some genuine encounters with this person, this father, called God – this father-God, who had sent his son on an inter-galactic, dimension-spanning mission to rescue and recycle me, to adopt me into his own royal family. I wanted to be a believer not a dealer or a debt enforcer. The struggle of wanting one life but experiencing another on a daily basis was too much for me, too hard for me to sustain. The problem was that I had tasted something different.

I wanted out.

I wanted a life where I didn't have to worry if there was spit in my food, or when Mum and Duke were coming back, or if I would ever hate her enough to lash out with my clenched fists.

I began to want something different.

*

The Cottage was the most amazing place. When we arrived in the big brown minibus, Maurice would switch off the engine and turn to us children in the back with his finger to his lips.

'Shhh. Listen, can you hear that?'

We would all fall silent and listen. The sound of absolutely nothing, almost complete silence, made my ears ring.

Someone would say, 'I can't hear anything. It's too quiet.'

'Exactly,' Maurice would reply. 'So, there's no need to shout here.'

They took us to nearby Wantage baths to swim. Maurice and Margaret played and splashed with us. They dunked us and sneaked up on us underwater. We tickled their feet and swam through their legs and showed off how far we could swim underwater.

We had crab apple fights in the garden, water fights with buckets and tubs, and tickle fights which always ended up with us getting 'the treatment' from Maurice's steely fingers in tender sides and ribs. We walked along country roads in the evenings as bats swooped and owls called. There was food like nowhere else – mountains and mountains of bread, ham, cheese, salad and cake; puddings and more puddings, and pies and casseroles, all eaten at a big table under low ceilings with birds singing outside and the cat sitting on the windowsill.

We would sing as Margaret played the guitar, songs of love and hope and streams of living water. Melodies dripping with fatherhood and adoption, peace and safety.

M&M knew that Mum was planning on travelling back to Jamaica and they knew that I did not want to go with her. One minute Mum loved what M&M did for me, taking me on holidays, getting me out of the house and from under her feet, the next minute they were brainwashing me and trying to steal me away. At one point there was amicable talk between Mum and M&M about the possibility of them looking after me while Mum went to Jamaica. Margaret spoke to me one day about it.

'I don't think you'd want us as parents. It would be difficult for you, you know? I don't think it would be as easy as you think.'

It didn't put me off. I didn't know how real a possibility it was in the grownup world, between the grownups, but in my mind the idea grew and grew. It was becoming easier and easier to spend time at M&M's flat, or at the Cottage. It was becoming harder and harder to spend time at home with Duke and Mum. I was treated more and more like a servant around the house. I was regularly sent on huge shopping errands to the supermarket down past Heman's Estate. The heavy bags made my fingers numb on the way back, two or three in each hand, making me stop and rest at intervals. There was always a drama with someone or something and Mum began to look increasingly to me to sort things out. And I bore a lot of the blame.

'This is your fault. If you were around more instead of swanning off to the club all the time I would get a little more help from you. You're old enough now. You're the man of the house.'

Duke was the man of the house and he was around less than I was now.

Mum knew she was losing me. She must have felt me slipping away.

I wanted school, learning, English, science. I had normal friends, with normal families who didn't want them to stay off school and help with the other children. I wanted to learn to play the guitar and excel at it. I wanted to be able to strum and pick and slide my fingers up and down the frets like I was Spanish. I wanted to read and write and walk through fields and woods. Mum could feel me slipping away, out of the concrete block, away from the hatred and mistrust.

I was standing on another threshold and I wanted to tip over and go in. One way or another, my days at Waldon Court with Mum and Duke and my two amazing sisters were coming to an end.

There must be at least fifty ways.

# 25

# ABANDONED NO MORE

'All the men in Mum's life abandoned her, including me.'

Dominic White, Christmas 2014.

*

I was at work when my sister called me. 'Mummy's in hospital. They don't think she's gonna survive this time Dominic. You'd better come quick if you can.'

I rushed to the train station and boarded the train to Waterloo. The taxi from the station to the hospital was painfully slow, too slow. I wondered if I would make it in time. It had been three hours plus since I had first received the call from my eldest sister.

When I arrived on the ward the first thing I saw were the security guards dealing with some people in the hall. They were trying to get past the big uniformed men to see someone. There was a teenage boy and two young women arguing and crying and shouting. As I went past them I had sight of who they were trying to get to. I only saw a glimpse but the young man was lying propped up, with tubes in his throat, and a blood-soaked white T-shirt ripped open exposing the wound. He had been shot or stabbed and doctors and nurses were milling around him while the man's friends or relatives argued in the corridor outside.

On I went to the cubicle where Mum lay, surrounded by my three sisters, all in floods of tears. We hugged and they cried and I sat holding Mum's pale hand in mine. She was unconscious but breathing, just – slowly, and laboured, but still alive. I was filled with immense disappointment. She couldn't see me and I couldn't see her. I could see her body. I could lift her eyelid if I'd wanted, but I would never again see the woman behind those green eyes. I had missed my chance.

I could touch her skin and caress her hand but she couldn't feel it. She didn't know it was me. Why do people wait until the last minute to try and reconnect with people whom they have shut out of their lives? Why did I do this? The machine bleeped as Mum's chest slowly rose and fell, her lungs gurgling with fluid. Why did I wait this long? What could I bring to this moment? What right even did I have to be there?

One of my daughters did meet my Mum and one of them didn't. My eldest daughter came with me and my wife on the train to London when she was two years old. We met my three sisters, their children, and Mum at a Mexican restaurant in Piccadilly and ate a meal together with beer, balloons, and laughter. Then we all went for a walk in St James Park with Mum hobbling around on her stick. We fed the ducks and ate ice-cream. Then we went to Trafalgar Square and played in the fountains bathed in sunshine. Finally we parted company. I went back to my life and Mum went back to hers.

I had not wanted to take my daughter to Mum's house. Previously I had visited Mum on my own and I had had to hold the door shut while Mum went to find the keys. A man on the other side was trying to get in. He had called Mum's name from outside causing Mum to spring into action.

'Quick Dougie, hold the door shut. Hold it tight and don't let him in. I need to get the key.'

By the time Mum came back with the key the man was yanking the handle and shouting to be let in over and over again.

'Mary! I know you is in there. Open the damn door now!'

'Mary!'

'Mary!'

I braced myself against the jerking handle as Mum finally managed to turn the key. The man eventually gave up and left. I did not want to take my wife or my daughters, to Mum's house.

My youngest daughter never had the opportunity to meet her grandmother. This is one of my biggest regrets for Mum and for my daughter. She knew that her elder sister had met Nana Mary and she wanted to meet her too. Every now and again she would remember and ask me.

'Daddy, when can we go and see Nana Mary and

your sisters?'

'Soon, we just need to arrange it.'

'But when though Daddy? It's not fair because I haven't ever met Nana Mary or your sisters. When Daddy, when?'

I kept saying that life was busy, time was short. Work was hard, money was tight. All true, but none of those reasons really stopped me from getting in the car or onto the train. Even not wanting to take my family to a house where safety was never guaranteed was no real excuse; there were ways around this, always ways.

The next time I saw my Mum after the Mexican meal was in hospital with my wife. At first we went straight past Mum's cubicle as I just didn't recognise her. She was so thin and frail, more like an old woman. Her chin was pointed and her face drawn but she was still smiling. Mum had just had major surgery. She had lost one failed kidney and had had a stent placed in her artery to keep the blood flowing. We laughed and joked with her while I couldn't believe how ravaged she was by sickness. I had spoken to her a few times on the phone but that was the last time I saw Mum conscious.

As I sat with her on her deathbed, watching as her breathing became slower and shallower, all of my cowardly choices and debilitating inadequacies surfaced. What right did I have to be with these fine young women who stuck with Mum all the way, who cried and wept bitterly for her as she lay dying?

We noticed that Mum's mouth was dry so we told

the nurse. A wet swab was brushed around the inside of her mouth, causing water to run down her chin. Soon after this machines began to bleep and Mum began her last struggle with life. She was a fighter, a survivor, and her approach to dying was no different. I placed my hand on her soft skin, just below her shoulder, and spoke into her face.

'We're all here Mum. We love you. Peace to you now Mum. You've done a good job. What a legacy you leave Mum, what a great legacy – three amazing daughters, a son, and eight beautiful grandchildren with another on the way. Well done Mum. We love you so much. I speak peace over you, Mum. I speak peace into you, Mum. Peace... Peace...' As she breathed her last breath I held on tightly to our bond, our skin-on-skin. I wanted her to know that I was close again.

Mary White died on the afternoon of Friday 14th January 2011 in a hospital bed in South London, surrounded by all four of her surviving children who stood together as she slipped away. She had fought through illness after illness including cancer, kidney failure, two heart attacks, a triple-bypass heart operation, diabetes and arteriosclerosis.

I would sit with you and bring my children to see your face. I would bring you as much peace as I possibly could to ease your fighting with this world, to help you in your struggle to survive.

All the men in Mary's life abandoned her, including me.

*

As I walked away from Mum peering out after me from the kitchen window, even then part of me wanted to turn back. But I had to kill that thought. I had to sever all ties in order to keep on walking. I had to abandon her, just like she had abandoned me. A portion of my heart turned to stone.

I went back to visit Mum many times over the following years, but mostly because I didn't want to lose connection with my sisters. My emotions towards her had become stony cold. When I was nineteen, I went back to live with Mum for a couple of months in the same flat, the same bedroom, in Waldon Court. I would read my now three sisters *The Magic Faraway Tree* and rock out with them in my bedroom to Nirvana playing 'Teen Spirit' and Blur whooping 'Song 2'. Eventually I left Mum again because her anger started to bubble up once more. I had refused to use physical force to get £20 from a lad two floors up who hadn't paid her for some coke. Eventually, I went up and asked for the money owed but came back empty-handed, which was an epic fail in Mum's book.

When I walked away from the kitchen window in 1985 I also abandoned my sisters. It was harder, much harder, to do it the second time when I was nineteen. I had never wanted to leave them.

Over the years, I lived out on a limb, separated from my family in a self-imposed exile. I seldom visited, sometimes going for more than a year without any contact. I wrote a few letters and phoned at times but often Mum would not have known where I was living or what I was doing, whether I was alive or dead.

I watched my sisters grow into young women only from a distance, in huge bursts of growth and change between my infrequent manifestations, missing huge chunks of their lives and struggles. One of the legacies of my choice to keep my distance from Mum was that I have not been there for my sisters. I have not allowed myself to be available for them, or known by them. I am always amazed at the grace they show towards me and the loving affection they have for me. In recent years, since Mum has died, I have had more contact with them than ever before, every moment of which has been precious to me.

In the days after Mum's death, I stayed with my eldest sister to help make arrangements for the funeral. In the morning her partner went to work and she got up to take her children to school, leaving me in the flat alone. I decided to do the washing up. On the stove, in a pan, sat some leftover Jamaican Brown Chicken – something I had not eaten since 1985. I sniffed it, inhaling deeply the familiar aroma, and then I ate every last bit of it.

It was like coming home.

At Mum's funeral on 3rd February 2011 at West Norwood Crematorium, an eclectic group of people sang hymns in thanksgiving and celebration of her life. I kept my bunch of roses by my side until the end of the service when family were allowed to go and see Mum in the coffin to pay their last respects. I offered my sisters and their children a rose each to place on her folded arms. I kept one back for myself. As I looked at Mum's pale face for the last time I lay my rose gently across her folded arms. It held all of her hopes and dreams. Many of her dreams had been fulfilled. I knew there were many good things she had enjoyed in life. I knew she loved her children and all of her grandchildren. But my rose was an acknowledgement of the heartache and pain that men had caused her. It was my last attempt at compensation. It represented the romance she had lacked, the self-giving that no man had fully bestowed upon her.

No man but one.

My rose represented the ultimate price that I knew had been paid for her two thousand years ago outside of a city's walls. My rose was a sign to her that His divine romance with her had never faded, never subsided – that there was a man who loved her without condition, without borders.

My rose was His rose, laid scarlet next to her pale skin.

*

As I was preparing for Mum's funeral, I listed all the songs I knew she had loved. I did not know all of Mum's favourites but I did know her favourite songs from a certain period of her life. I sat and listened to each one on Youtube, sometimes over and over again. 'Many Rivers to Cross', 'Johnny Remember Me', 'Streets of London', 'Blinded by the Light', 'Scarborough Fair', 'Mr Bo-Jangles', 'Fifty Ways'. I was back with her in Martin Street while she ironed and sang. I was back with her in Granny's yard in Jamaica as Mary and Eli swayed together in the starlight. I was back with Mum through her music.

This was the first time I had rolled the stone away from the emotional grave within – a grave where I had buried my feelings for Mum. I had mistakenly thought they were dead. But feelings, if buried, are buried alive.

The music took me to places I had been unwilling to go. When I left Mum in the kitchen, she had to be all bad, all wrong. She had to hate me, with no trace of love left. After all the years of my own ever-living hope being dashed and bruised and broken, and yet remaining alive, it had to finally die. I had to discount all of the good things about Mum, all of the things that might stop me from abandoning her.

I had to finally stop holding on.

But the music took me back to the motorbike, to the Cornish beach, to the flat near Nottingham Castle, with the sweet smells and the purring cat, to the faraway Jamaican shores beside the glistening Caribbean Sea. To the woman with green eyes and soft skin.

Then, two years later, I decided to write a book.

If I had wanted to remain aloof and cold towards Mum, to keep all of those shining memories buried in the tomb, writing a book was my worst mistake. As I went back to the knife, and the guitar, I had to go back further and lift the lid on what lay hidden beneath. I had to meet again the woman who loved cats and the boy who danced on a beach with his mother thinking he was doing Kung Fu.

I had to let the pain of loss wash over me, the torn bonds of attachment slipping out of my grasp.

I had to climb back onto your motorbike, press my face into your back and smile. I had to grab your leather jacket and pull myself close to you.

'Hold on tight, Dougie!'

'Okay, Mum.'

# POSTSCRIPT

I knew from the start that this memoir would be about our relationship and what we both chose to do with it. What I did not know was that it would bring to life feelings long buried - my love for her and my appreciation of all the good which she brought to me. I have described the process of my journey to family and friends as like setting off to hunt for scarce diamonds in a coalmine but instead finding a cavern full of glistening gems. Writing has reawakened all my good memories as well as my bad ones, but there are far more good memories than I could have ever have hoped for.

It has had an impact upon me. I can't say for sure exactly what because it is still echoing and resonating through my life, through my soul and spirit. I will no doubt be able to describe the impact of the process of rediscovering my childhood bonds with my mum more fully in the years to come. I hope it will help me to become a better husband, father, friend; a more whole and well-rounded person. Time will tell.

If you had asked me about my childhood before I began writing I would have offered statements like, 'it's all relative,' or, 'well, it's all I ever knew so it wasn't that bad really'. The truth is I had very little understanding of my own childhood, of what I had experienced. Even now I would describe this memoir as only the beginning of understanding. It is the beginning of the answer to the question, 'what was my childhood like?'

I would not have been able to write this with such confidence had it not been for records faithfully kept by professionals during the mid to late 1970s in Derbyshire County Council. These people told my story from their own unique and adult perspective, a viewpoint far removed from my own child-level observance. Their narrative of my life has added a richness of understanding to my own. After writing to Derbyshire County Council to request access to my records I received a letter from the Service Manager on 6th April 2009 stating 'I can confirm some records have been found.' On 24th April 2009, one day after my thirty-eighth birthday, I finally received a letter from Derbyshire County Council stating that they were satisfied that I had provided sufficient proof that I was indeed me. A few weeks later my records arrived in a plain brown A4 sized envelope which was surprisingly thin. Inside was a buff-coloured folder containing my notes. The first page read, 'T3370. Name: White Dominic Justin.' That was my number, there before me in black and white.

I sat and opened and read. And read. And read. When I had finished I passed the records to my wife who also read and read. Then, when she had finished reading, I put them back into the envelope and placed it in my keepsake shoe box at the bottom of my wardrobe. They remained there under my dangling shirts for more than two years.

They were pondered and discussed from time to time but the sheets of photocopied paper remained in the shoe box. It took me a while to even begin to process my thoughts about what had been written about me. I had always thought that my abandonment as a child, by my mother, was my fault. There must have been something bad or unlovely about me that led to my mum deciding that she would rather leave me in the care of other people. Even as an adult this feeling lingered even though I knew with my rational mind that this was not true. The feeling still lingered that it was my fault. The thing that started to shift this grey veil for me was reading what other grownups had said about Mum and I, and the bond between us - social workers and teachers, residential care staff, doctors. It started to sink in slowly. *It wasn't my fault.*

After leaving the yeast of these thoughts to slowly rise I retrieved my notes from the shoe box and began to reread them for a second, third, fourth and fifth time. I saw things I had previously missed, gems of insight hidden away in the dusty narrative of reports and Reception into Care notes. I began to hang disjointed memories on the backbone of the timeline. Suddenly I could know exactly when I stopped wetting the bed, where I was when my best friend knocked me out cold with one well-timed punch. I could confidently piece all of the fragments together to make a whole. I could see a story emerging, my story, which in time became our story.

I began to take notes from my records dated from 20th May 1976 to 26th September 1980. My pen inked those first words into a brown leather-bound notebook in May 2013 while my wife was on an international trip away from home for a week. After breakfast and the school run I read and wrote. I retrieved children from school, cooked tea, washed hair and read bedtime stories. Then I returned to the desk under our bedroom window with a view of suburbia and I wrote into the night, only crawling into bed after my cheek had touched the desk with the lolling of my sleepy head.

I continued writing when I could snatch moments in the busyness of life but in the summer holidays of 2013 I realised that progress with the book was coming too slowly. So, after getting the okay from my family, I asked my boss for a day off.

'Please can I have Mondays off?'

'What do you want the time off for?'

'To write a book – It's going to be a memoir of my early childhood.'

'That sounds like an interesting project. Well, other people in the team already work flexitime so there's no reason why you shouldn't.'

'Thanks.'

'No problem.'

And that was that - four long days working as a Social Services Assistant in the Youth Offending Service and one day a week writing my memoir. Monday was my Mr Ben day when as if by magic the shopkeeper appeared and out from the changing room I stepped with my brown book and fine-line pen in hand. I revisited streets and houses I had not seen for years. I remembered how my mum had smelt with her white-musk perfume and leather jackets laden with cold, fresh air. I remembered how other people had smelt - some dank odours I had almost managed to forget. On my Mondays I became an author for twelve months, a year of my life spent recalling suppressed memories through reading notes and compiling lists. Some memories were retrieved easily whilst others still hang back at the very edge of recollection. They hang like an unseen shadow just beyond my reach, perhaps remaining there as a measure of self protection.

When I had typed up the first draft it read like a Court report. These are the facts, when this happened, followed by this with this person and that with someone else. I write court reports for a living (among other things) so this was no surprise. I had the working title of *The Real Life Adventures of Cat Lady and the Kung Fu Kid*. I knew that at some point this would have to change; it sounded too much like a comic novel.

Then I began to redraft my report, finding a beginning and middle, unearthing the story as I brushed away the soil and dirt of the facts. My own narrative began to take shape and substance, more and more with every new draft. It increasingly became an emotional journey as I reconnected with the little brown-haired boy and the crazy, powerful green-eyed woman. Feelings which I thought were dead began to come back to life. There were times I thought that I could feel my mum in the room with me, peering over my shoulder observing my words, sentences and paragraphs as they dripped from my fingers. This was especially true during my writing of the closing chapters, which were not present in the earlier drafts. I did not know how I was going to loop the narrative back to the start until it actually happened. When the last chapter finally came it was accompanied by hot tears long kept at bay.

In the beginning this memoir was going to be about me and what happened to me, and how I felt, but that wasn't the story which I found. It wasn't about me; it was about us - us and the fragile bond between us. This story came alive under my fingers and pulled me in. At times it has consumed most of my waking thoughts and drained my emotional energy. I thank my family for allowing me to travel on this journey and for living with me while my attention has been divided.

Finding a title for this book was the hardest part for me. It wasn't about Kung Fu. It wasn't just about me, or just about Mum, so I did not want to simply call it *The Cat Lady*. That does not adequately sum her up anyway.

I removed the euphemism which had served its purpose in leading me into the narrative flow. What remained was the substance of the book, what it was really about. What I found was a story of a son's search for his mother's love - attachment, love-chemicals, maternal bonds broken and reformed, and the closeness of my mother's skin. Then I remembered the journey in the night on the back of my mum's motorbike. I remembered holding tightly to her leather jacket. I remembered how comforting it felt to press my face into her leather-clad back. We had to be close to each other on that motorbike, just like we had been at my birth and in the swimming pool before I had learned to swim.

This book ends when I chose to leave, when I stopped holding on.

It is tempting for me to begin to tell the next chapter of my life which followed my decision to leave my home - tempting because it feels like it needs 'airing', cleaning out my closet, just like Marshall Mathers. But I won't do that here because that story ceases to be about me and Mum.

The next chapter is about me after I stopped holding on to Mum, and that is a completely different adventure altogether.

# ABOUT THE AUTHOR

Dominic J White is a husband, father, and writer. To fund all of those three pursuits he works with teenagers who have been caught breaking the law. As a former looked-after-child he has a good general appreciation of issues which affect children, teenagers and adults who have experienced a Local Authority as their guardian.

Dominic was born in Derby, UK, and moved to Jamaica when he was nine years old where he lived for six months. After learning patois he went on to spend his teenage years in Brixton, South-West London, where he enjoyed roller-skating and visits to the West End when he should have been at school.

He enjoys writing reports for the Court, writing memoirs, and planning his next book. Most of all, he enjoys spending time with his family where he is outnumbered three to one in regards to gender. Favourite pastimes for Dominic and his family are holidays in Cornwall, camping, walking, and reading. He is a man of faith, and refuses to believe that the moon is the perfect size due to mere chance.

He lives and writes in Southampton, Hampshire, where he would one day like to own a leather-bound armchair, beside his much dreamed-of writer's desk, in which he can comfortably seat children, teenagers and adults alike.

Dominic J White has a paternal Greek-Cypriot heritage, and he suspects that his biological father has brown eyes and an olive complexion, much like himself and his two daughters.

www.dominicjwhite.com

www.facebook.com/dominicjwhiteauthor

www.twitter.com/domjwhite

www.twitter.com/jamaicankungfu

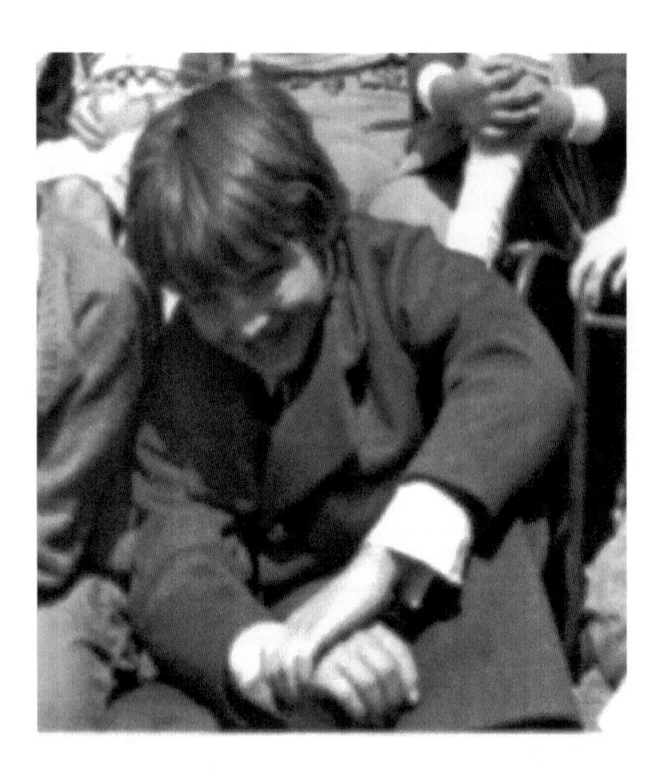